It's Not About Math, It's About Life

by
Kari Simmons Kling

It's Not About Math, It's About Life

by Kari Simmons Kling
Karen Olsen, Editor and Contributor

© 1997 Susan J. Kovalik
Printed in the United States of America

ISBN 1-878631-33-0

Illustrations: Daniel Fisch, Andrew Larsen, Jeremy McNeely,
Jordan McNeely, Matthew McNeely, Mary West
Graphics and Layout: Kristina Roe

Published by Susan Kovalik & Associates

Distributed by Books For Educators, Inc.
17051 SE 272nd St., Suite 18
Kent, WA 98042-4959
Toll Free: 888/777-9827 Fax: 253/630-7215
www.books4educ.com

Dedicated to the memory
and spirit of my brother,

Jeffrey L. Bishop, Ph.D.

for teaching me to reach
for the stars

Table of Contents

TABLE OF CONTENTS

Acknowledgments

To my parents (all four of them) and the rest of my family, you have always believed in me and have told me that I could achieve anything that I set my mind to. Your unconditional support cannot be measured.

To Karen Olsen, whose talents, skills, and patience have taken my ways of thinking to a much higher level than I ever thought possible. This book would never have been completed without you.

To Susan Kovalik, your commitment, your passion, and your generosity have made the world a better place for children everywhere. Thank you for recognizing capabilities I possessed before I recognized them myself.

To Kristina Roe, thank you for caring about this book as though it were your own.

To all of you out there who responded, "Sure!" whenever I asked, "Would you mind filling out a short survey?" or "Would you mind reading this and telling me what you think?" I hesitate to try to name you individually. There are far too many of you and I wouldn't want to leave anyone out. Please accept my heartfelt thanks for caring enough to take the time to participate. This book will be much more useful to its readers because of your feedback.

For the title of this book, thank you to Susan Kovalik and to Joy Raboli for recognizing that it *was* a title.

To my young illustrators, your generation will benefit from your contribution to this book.

And to my husband and best friend, Bobby Kling, your never-ending encouragement, support, and understanding of my passion for my life's work is a gift to me on a daily basis.

From the Author

When I first began to think about writing a book about math education, I asked myself the following questions over and over, "Who am I kidding? Why am I writing a book about math? I was never a good math student in school, I wasn't a math major in college. I needed a tutor to survive statistics in graduate school! I don't think like a mathematician, nor can I compute in my head like one!"

After much reflection, I decided these are exactly the reasons why I should write such a book. A great majority of, if not almost all, books on the market relating to mathematics education in this country, have been written by "pure mathematicians." Ahh, perhaps this is our problem? Most of us don't think like pure mathematicians, nor can we perform like them, yet the literature written by them expects us to do so. I don't believe that thinking like pure mathematicians is a natural way of thinking for a great majority of the population and it distracts us from our real purpose as teachers in elementary schools: to make students effective users of mathematics in the real world.

This book is written for those of you who suffer math anxieties, phobias, or perceived mathematical inadequacies. It is time to no longer feel ashamed. It is my hope that this book allows you to reassess your fears or to validate your successes in regard to math, while offering hope to those teachers who feel they can never teach above a certain grade level because of "the math." I encourage you to go for it!

Kari Kling
January, 1997
Scottsdale, AZ

Chapter 1
Introduction

As a young child, I did anything to avoid math. I would literally become sick on a day I knew I had a math test or, failing that, pretend to be sick during math so that I could escape to the nurse's office. My elementary school memories of "arithmetic" class (we didn't even call it math much less mathematics) are filled with emotion and panic. I can vividly recall numerous times I was asked to go to the chalkboard, by myself, and work out an arithmetic problem in front of the entire class. Most times, my attempts were unsuccessful and I learned to live with the shame that I felt because "I was not very good at 'rithmetic."

Junior high school brought new hopes that my outlook about that subject having to do with numbers would improve. It didn't. My teachers asked me to figure out percentages, ratios, and averages, while I was trying to figure out when and how this would affect my life. More confusion and wonder about numbers, their meaning, and their relevance to my own life continued.

Although my computational abilities did improve in high school, my understanding of how and where to apply the theorems and algorithms did not. I became knowledgeable about how to do the calculations even though I never admitted that I had no idea what they meant. For example, it wasn't until I took statistics in graduate school that I finally understood when to use different algebraic formulas and why. I believe the reason for this understanding was that I finally had had experiences using the content; as a teacher over a ten-year period I gave standardized tests to my students and then had to interpret them. After application to real world situations, it was finally making sense. I realized

"Dear Kari, Enjoyed having you in class, too bad you didn't do better."

(message in my high school senior yearbook from my math teacher)

"Life is change. Growth is optional. Choose wisely."

-Karen Kaiser Clark

that it was almost impossible for me to understand the application of the skills learned without having a "being there" experience first. Once I had the experience, I was able to see how the pieces were supposed to fit into the big picture. Looking back, I know I was not alone in my confusion.

It wasn't surprising to me that when I became an educator, math never seemed to be an area I was eager to delve into. Fortunately, I worked with a group of educators who were helpful and supportive. I began to be a real "kid watcher,"[1] observing other successful educators, immersing myself in staff development, and reading about the "mysteries of math." But most importantly, I began to carefully observe how and where mathematical concepts were applied in my everyday life. Slowly, I began to see relationships, patterns began to emerge, connections were being made, and I was beginning to see the world differently.

Once I was able to see the connections, I knew that I had to orchestrate learning so that my students could understand the language of mathematics and its interconnectedness to the rest of the curriculum and the world. Simply teaching arithmetic skills was not enough. "In reality, no one can teach mathematics. Effective teachers are those who can stimulate students to learn mathematics. Educational research offers compelling evidence that students learn mathematics well only when they construct their own mathematical understanding."[2]

This last statement sends an important message. It implies that unless we provide opportunities for our students to use mathematical concepts to solve problems important to them and thus construct their own mathematical understandings, we are not effectively teaching mathematics; we are simply filling our students with isolated bits and pieces of information about numbers which alone will not lead to mathematical literacy. Galileo once said, "You cannot teach people anything. You can only help them discover it within themselves." Our job as professional educators must be to provide opportunities for students to be actively engaged in problem solving that is interconnected with what is happening on a daily basis in the classroom and that mirrors real life.

My purpose in writing this book is to help classroom teachers explore their own mathematical understanding and examine how it is translated into his or her math curriculum, while reflecting on the application of these skills in the world. Math should not be taught only at "math time" but should be used throughout the day as it pertains to real life. Math is everywhere! We use math in science, in language arts, in the social sciences, in the creative arts, in sports, at mealtime, at recess, at play, at home, at school, at the doctor's office, the airport, the grocery store, the newspaper, EVERYWHERE! Until we, as adults, can see the interrelatedness of mathematics and how it influences so much of what we do on a daily basis, we cannot provide the kinds of learning opportunities students need and deserve. We cannot provide what we don't possess—an active understanding of math in the real world.

Many people, including many educators, use the terms "arithmetic" and "mathematics" as though they mean the same thing. They decidedly do not! Arithmetic refers to the addition, subtraction, multiplication, and division of numbers; the computation piece. Mathematics refers to the bigger picture: the conceptual understanding of numbers and how they relate to one another, revealing hidden patterns that help us understand the world around us. Arithmetic, if you will, is a part of mathematics and a necessary part. However, by itself it does not assist students in the process of understanding their world. If you were to take a magic peek into every teacher's lesson plan book in America, the listed assignment/activity during "math time" would most likely be a computation lesson. "Mathematics as commonly presented in today's elementary schools has been described as a 'curriculum out of balance.' Researchers point to a heavy emphasis on rote mastery of computational skills on the one hand and scant attention to creatively exploring mathematical concepts derived from the child's everyday experiences on the other."[3] As educators, we have become better at teaching arithmetic but we need to recognize the need to teach more mathematics as well as to improve our teaching of it.

I have been a classroom teacher for the past fourteen years. For the past five years, I have had the privilege of working with fellow educators as a staff development trainer and consultant focusing on how to apply recent brain research to our classrooms and schools using the Kovalik ITI Model. When exploring the subject of curriculum integration, the same question always arises: "How am I supposed to integrate math?" Invariably, the teachers I worked with considered math to be the last and most difficult subject to integrate. That is absolutely true if we look at teaching math the way it is typically done, i.e. "Open your book and turn to page 45. Do problems 1-15." Under such circumstances it would be most difficult to integrate such assignments because they address isolated skills, mostly computational. According to Leslie Hart, "The old notion of 'teach a lesson now, students learn a lesson now' plainly doesn't work in today's schools once we go beyond rote."[4]

On the other hand, if we focus on the concepts of mathematics AND if we are teaching subjects like science or social studies using real life locations ("slices of real life"), the integration of mathematics and the attainment of conceptual, as well as computational, understanding becomes much easier. As one recovering math-phobic teacher commented, "All you need to integrate math are numbers and statistics about the real world things you are studying. How big, how many, how heavy, how far, how fast, how many years ago, etc.?"

This is not a "how to" book for integrating math; it is a book about how to make the learning of math accessible to all students. It is my hope that the words on these pages will serve as a springboard for teachers to incorporate math concepts into their daily curriculum in ways that will be meaningful, relevant, and full of application opportunities. Susan Kovalik states that, "The human brain will only learn and retain what is perceived as being meaningful and the person who decides what is meaningful is the learner." Keeping that thought in mind, it is not surprising that our textbooks present and represent the same mundane facts year after year and yet the kids aren't getting it.

Without purpose, from the students' perspective, for computation, students are not able to realize the interconnectedness and purpose of what they are learning and how that fits into their lives outside of school. By basing curriculum in the study of a slice of real, frequently visitable life, we can provide that cognitive framework for our students that makes mathematics understandable and useable to them and we can at the same time easily and naturally integrate our curriculum.

So, welcome to a new view of math appreciation, understanding, and application. It has been a long time coming. Whether you are a kindergarten teacher, a high school teacher, or an administrator, I encourage you to reassess your own thinking regarding math education. It is up to us to reevaluate what we want our students to know and how these skills and concepts will positively impact their lives. "We need to be challenged to think for ourselves and to become aware of the mathematical possibilities of the environment. If we are to spark children's mathematical imaginations, we must first rekindle our own."[5]

Remember, it's not about math; it's about life!

Chapter 2
Real Math vs.
School Math
—OR—
Math Anxiety: Everything you ever wanted to know but were too anxious to ask

Math anxiety is very real. It is a fear that usually begins in childhood and remains with a person for a lifetime. In fact, over the past twenty years, math-anxiety reduction clinics have been established in many colleges and continuing education programs around the country. For me and many others, most math in school can be almost paralyzing. Even today, if I am asked to figure out a problem, even though I know that I have the ability to solve it, my first reaction is still filled with emotion. In fact, "recent research on math anxiety has shown the phenomenon to be real and to have an impact on people's perceptions of themselves and of their career choices."[1] Math anxiety is real and it can be crippling.

PREVENTING MATH ANXIETY

The causes of math anxiety are many but four culprits stand out: mixed messages, artificiality and lack of relevance, tracking and long-term grouping, and standardized testing.

Problem #1: Mixed Messages

If students are baffled by the question "What is mathematics?" they are not alone. In her book, *Fear of Math: How to Get Over It and Get On With Your Life*, Claudia Zaslavsky reviews some of the common misconceptions about math. Broadly shared by students, teachers, parents, and society in general, they include:

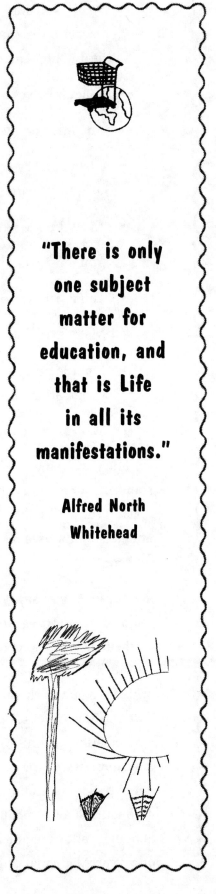

"There is only one subject matter for education, and that is Life in all its manifestations."

Alfred North Whitehead

- Math is mainly arithmetic, working with numbers. If you are not good in arithmetic, for example you haven't memorized the multiplication tables, you can't learn "higher level" math such as algebra and calculus.

- Math involves a lot of memorization of facts, rules, formulas, and procedures.

- You must follow the procedures set down by the teacher and the textbook.

- Math must be done fast. If you can't solve a problem in a few minutes, you might as well give up.

- Every problem has just one right answer, and it must be exact.

- You must work on math alone. Working with other people is cheating.

- You must keep at it until you have solved the problem.

- Math is hard. Only a genius or a "math brain" can understand it.

- Math language is rigid, uncreative, cut-and-dried, complete. It doesn't involve imagination, discovery, invention. There is nothing new in math.

- Math is exact, logical, and certain. Intuition doesn't enter into it.[2]

You may or may not agree with all of the misconceptions above or perhaps you have some of your own to add to the list. Whatever the case, misconceptions about real mathematics caused by the version of math taught in schools, "school math," confound our attempts to improve the teaching of math and leave students wondering "What's going on here?"

But wait, you say. What about those students who enjoy math and choose to take math courses? These students are doing just fine. They are the people that become our mathematicians and choose careers that rely highly on mathematical skills. Maybe, but we are still losing many of these students as well. We must accept that our traditional arithmetic approach serves no one. In *Everybody Counts: A Report to the Nation on the Future of Mathematics Education,* the evidence is clear: half of our students drop out of the mathematics pipeline every year, never to take another math course. The report is honest in its appraisal of the causes: "More than any other subject, mathematics filters students out of programs leading to scientific and professional careers. From high school through graduate school, the half-life of students in the mathematics pipeline is about one year, although various requirements hold some students in class temporarily for an extra term or a year. Mathematics is the worst curricular villain in driving students to failure in school."[3] You may be wondering why I am making reference to high school and graduate school when this book is primarily geared to elementary and middle school. The reason is clear. Opinions and abilities regarding math and math anxiety do not begin in high school. I believe they begin in the early years. We must show children the true connections between school math and real math throughout all the school years, building on the knowledge children already have when they come to us in kindergarten.

Possible solutions to problem #1. Narrowing the real math versus school math dichotomy is the first step to improving achievement in mathematics. For our students' sake and for our own sanity, we must re-examine our definition of mathematics education. Perhaps our school's curriculum is too simplistic and incomplete, perhaps expectations of students are too low, or, more likely, our implementation does not match our written curriculum. Or, perhaps all of the above are involved.

State and national frameworks, as well as numerous publications, can help us solve the problems of a definition that is too simplistic or incomplete while providing us with a vision of what appropriate expectations should be. (See Chapter 3 for a discussion of what mathematics is and resources for developing curriculum.) It is also helpful to keep in mind that when most students arrive at our classroom doorstep, even as early as kindergarten, they already have a vast amount of knowledge about the world around them. This includes mathematical concepts. "Schools generally ignore the fact that children enter school with a considerable amount of mathematical knowledge, picked up from their families and the environment, and processed by means of their own problem-solving abilities, just as they acquired language."[4] I have yet to meet an entering kindergarten student that has told me they suffered from math anxiety or that they "weren't very good in math." Clearly the breakdown begins early in schools and continues throughout the grades.

If, however, the problem is that our implementation doesn't match our written curriculum, the solutions will require more effort because the job requires not just taking on new perspectives and actions but, more hazardously and difficult, leaving old ideas and materials and habits of mind behind. In other words, the problem is not just what is missing but also what is present, old ways of "doing math" that hinder rather than help us and our students.

What is missing is the use of the real world (as students experience it) as the source of problems to be analyzed and solved, problems whose answers mean something to students, that excite them and bring greater meaning to what they are learning about. Like reading, math for citizens of the 21st century is a means to an end, not an end in itself. Not

"A widespread misconception about mathematics is that it is completely hierarchical— first arithmetic, then algebra, then calculus, then more abstraction, then whatever.... This belief in the totem pole nature of mathematics isn't true but it prevents many people who did poorly in seventh grade, high school, or even college mathematics from picking up a popular book on the subject."

John Allen Paulous

until university levels should the study of math be considered an end in itself. For elementary students, it should be considered a tool for unlocking greater understandings of the world in which we live. Math isn't something we do to numbers; math is a thinking process that helps us understand more about the world around us than we could know without the use of those tools. Math is a fundamental literacy for citizenship.

Mathematics affect us in our lives at many different levels, each of which should be included in our math instruction:[5]

- Practical—figuring unit prices in the supermarket, understanding the effects of inflation, balancing a bank account, helping the kids with their homework, applying for a loan.

- Civic—understanding such public policy issues as tax rates, the education budget, health care, preserving the environment, and the effect of racism, sexism, and other forms of discrimination.

- Professional—applies to fields ranging from business management and health care to mechanics and physics.

- Leisure—games of chance and games of strategy, puzzles, and prediction and analysis of sports events.

- Cultural—the role of mathematics as a major intellectual tradition, as a subject appreciated as much for its beauty as for its power. Like language, religion, and music, mathematics is a universal part of human culture. All societies throughout the ages have developed mathematical ideas and practices appropriate to their needs and interests.

Problem #2: Artificiality and Irrelevance

The scenario is familiar, from our own experiences and those of our children and grandchildren, pages and pages of computation drills erratically interrupted by those dreaded word problems.

The pluses, take aways, times, and gozintas (goes into) of computation drills too often involve disembodied numbers, big and small that never offer a sense of what is happening or why—naked numbers, devoid of context and meaning, cold, distant, and irrelevant. As a result, students leave us with little sense of number-ness—an inner sense of approximately how much the result of the computation should be. Did the finger slip or could 21 x 99 equal 207,900? Does sales tax of $9.73 on a $50 portable radio sound about right? Perhaps more importantly, does the student even care?

Word problems, or story problems, are often considered the pièce 'de resistance, the key to making math relevant for students. In theory they could be, but in practice, they typically suffer from one or both of two common ailments. As Michael Smith points out, "textbook 'story problems' are worded in such a way that children learn to look for key words. For example, 'left' in a problem means subtraction. It isn't even necessary to read the whole problem; just subtract the smaller number from the larger number. Besides, every problem on the page is done exactly the same way. No need to think at all! It doesn't take long for children to internalize the idea that understanding has no relationship to school math."[6] Unfortunately, mathematics in real life is seldom so obvious and simple and such artificial examples are viciously misleading.

Furthermore, many story problems use fragments of real life in a phony way. Three examples from Michael K. Smith's book, *Humble Pi: The Role Mathematics Should Play in School*, are illustrative:

1. Sam can do a job in five hours working by himself. Bill, however, can do it in three hours. How long will it take them if they work together?

2. Jonathan can bicycle from his home to school in 12 minutes while his older sister Suzanne can make the same trip in eight minutes. If Jonathan starts from home to school at the same time that Suzanne starts from school to home, how long will it be before they meet?

3. Miguel is eight years older than his brother, Juan. Five years from now, he will be twice as old as Juan. How old are the boys now?

As Smith comments, "although all three examples have 'algebraic solutions,' how sensible are the assumptions that we must make to find the correct answer? When two people work together on a task, simple psychology indicates that the time to complete it depends on many factors. Similarly, when two people start out on a trip, a time when they will meet is contingent on several things. For anyone who has lived a normal life, these last two statements are only common sense. Finally, concerning the age problem, how many people would not know the ages of their own brothers?"[7] If it weren't so absurd that these were the kinds of problems that we were asking students to solve, they would be pretty funny. Sadly, they do nothing to make math come alive for students.

Possible solutions to problem #2. Mathematics is not a luxury, a hobby for the rich, or a pastime for the eccentric. An understanding of mathematics is a necessary area of expertise for a citizenry to make informed decisions in the ballot box, balance a checkbook, and handle the family budget.

"Look at some of the challenges we face. Global warming, destruction of the protective ozone layer, ocean pollution, destruction of the tropical rain forest, air pollution, extinction of animal and plant species, groundwater pollution, urban crowding, exhaustion of natural resources, desertification, drug-resistant disease organisms, aging populations, expanding slums, widespread poverty, global economic imbalance, increasing crime, increasing demands for energy and other resources, and ever-faster absolute population growth. Our choices, individual and collective, deliberate and habitual, totaling trillions a day, carry us relentlessly on. We can never revisit the status quo ante.

Understanding such challenges requires the ability to comprehend large numbers, to know what they count or measure; to understand rates, rates of change, and accelerated rates of change; to estimate; to gauge time; to forecast; and to preview how the changes may affect our lives. In short, just to grasp the nature of the challenges we face requires considerable mathsemantic sophistication."[8]

Thus, it is critical that we model math as an everyday experience for everyone. To do so, we must begin by allowing students to be able to see and experience the math in the things they do and places they go to each day. Basing math instruction on multiple real experiences beyond the classroom is an absolute must (see Chapter 10). It is our job as teachers to plan such study trips to ensure a common experiential base for math instruction.

We must be clear: artificiality confuses the brain and irrelevance kills attention and motivation to learn, making it extremely difficult for the human brain—at all ages—to move information from short-term to long-term memory. As recent brain research makes clear, the brain demands that the content and skills it is asked to learn be meaningful and useful. Relevance as used here means real to the student's life, involving matters he or she can intuitively grasp, understand, appreciate, care about, see himself or herself doing. And because the experiences children bring with them to school vary so markedly, the only real-life experiences we can depend upon to be meaningful to all students are those we provide through the study of a nearby location or event that we have selected to serve as the basis for our study of science, social studies, etc. Using the student's experiences of such locations and events is an effective way to ensure understanding of the dreaded story problem. By creating story problems that come directly from such experiences, and/or allowing them to construct their own problems, in relation to what is being experienced, students will have a greater chance of understanding the math concepts and their application. The teacher plays a crucial role in orchestrating this type of learning.

For example, if your classroom or your school operates a school store, the following problems could be generated:

- If school tee shirts cost $12.00 per shirt, how many shirts must you sell to reach a gross total sales goal of $432.00? What is the cost of manufacturing each tee shirt? Does the cost go down if the quantity goes up? How much do you have to sell the shirts for in order to make a profit of 10%, 20%, or 30%?

- If the class recycling project sells at least one bag of aluminum cans every Friday for $5.00, how many weeks would it take to save $80 after paying collection cost of $2.00 per bag? (Stay awake here, remainders are inappropriate as part of the answer!)

- You go to the class store with $2.25 worth of coupons to redeem. On this particular day, the store is redeeming coupons for triple their value. How much money would you save today?

- Your student store is considering offering credit for major purchases—3% payable in 30 days. If you bought a $17 item and paid your credit line off in 30 days, how much extra would the item cost you? What item in the store could you have bought for that cost?

Story problems based upon a study of a slice of life, in this case, a location well suited to the study of systems (economics and recycling) are ever powerful because they are real life problems not simulations.

- On your study trip to the local grocery store, you discover that the store's net profit is only two cents on the dollar. The store takes in an average of $23,000 per day. What is their profit for one day, a month, a year?

- This same grocery store suffers from a high rate of shoplifting. On average, the store loses $500 a day. If they could cut shoplifting in half, what would their profit be for one day, a month, a year?

- Find an environmentally unfriendly, overpackaged item in the store. Figure the cost per ounce. Next find these same items in inexpensive, environmentally-friendly packaging. Compute their cost per ounce (do your best to guesstimate similar quantities of each of the contents). How much would you save if you purchased the same contents of approximately the same quantity if packaged in an environmentally-friendly way? Show your work.

Extension #1: If your family ate an average of five pounds a month of these foods, how much would your family save by buying in an environmentally-friendly way?

Extension #2: How many months before the manufacturer/distributor of the environmentally-unfriendly product lost $50 in sales to your family? What would the loss be if all the families represented by your class purchased similarly?

Extension #3: Write a letter to the manufacturer/distributor of the product and share your information with them.

A sense of numbers—an intuitive sense of what their quantity represents—is essential if math is to "come alive" for students. Without it, numbers in the newspaper, on the job, in the voting booth, or in the classroom are meaningless and do not help extract perspective or meaning from the situation. This is as true for the family member responsible for budgeting and shopping for groceries as for the university higher math student. (For a discussion of developing a sense of number or N-ness, see *"Anchor" Math: The Brain-Compatible Approach to Learning Math* by Leslie Hart.)[9] To develop that sense of number-ness, students need lots of opportunities to quantify and analyze objects in their own realm of experience. They must understand the mathematics from their experiences in the environment they interact with on a daily basis before they can understand mathematics in the larger world, more distant from personal experience, more abstract. Problems such as those at the class and grocery stores above help students get a sense of numbers and what they mean to their personal lives.

Problem #3: Tracking and Long-Term Grouping

Another significant contributor to fear and avoidance of mathematics is tracking and the dread of long-term assignment to the "dummy" group. I am sad to report that in many schools, children are already tracked by the beginning of first grade. These decisions are usually made on the recommendations of the kindergarten teacher, a score from a standardized test and/or teacher observation. The decision to track students in schools is made many times because it is more convenient for teachers, not necessarily because it is in the best interest of our children. We must change our focus as educators to that of teaching children (student-driven, real-life) and not simply that of teaching the curriculum (text-driven).

When reflecting on tracking in my own schooling, I am reminded of a painful childhood memory. My earliest recollections regarding tracking are from the second grade. There were four teachers in the grade level and each teacher taught a different ability group (low, low-average, high-average, and high). We were affectionately known as "Group 1, Group 2, Group 3, and Group 4." Group 1 were the "academic superstars" and Group 4 were the students who were known as "just a little bit slower." I distinctly remember these groups as being the "social classes" of our grade level. On the playground, most of us only associated with those in our group. This scenario continued throughout our elementary years.

During the first year of being tracked, I was one of the fortunate students: I was placed in Group 1, the high group. This was probably due to the fact that I was a very good reader, which I believe overshadowed the fact that I was just "O.K." in arithmetic. I remained in Group 1 for four and one-half years. I can remember always wondering about what "those other kids" were like and what they did

> "For most people, mathematics is more than a subject. It is a relationship between themselves and a discipline purported to be "hard" and reserved only for an elite and powerful few."
>
> Sheila Tobias

in their classes. I found out in the sixth grade. Sixth grade meant a lot of things, my first "grown up" dress (my description, not my mothers. . .), my first sleep-over birthday party, and LONG DIVISION! I had an extremely difficult time understanding this concept. Even with the additional help provided to me by my math teacher and my parents, I just couldn't seem to get it.

The more people tried to help me, the more worried I became, the more frustrated I got, the less I could do. If only I understood then about the triune brain and the power of emotions to override the functioning of the cerebral cortex. I continued to blame myself for being so stupid, and then it happened. I was being moved. The teachers had decided that it would be in my best interest for me to change groups. I was no longer a member of Group 1, I had been demoted to Group 3! I felt I would be stigmatized forever! I was doing well in all of my other classes, but no one seemed to know what to do with this kid who just couldn't 'get' long division. The other groups were ready to go on, and I was apparently holding them up. As you can imagine, this would be traumatic for any sixth grader. I can still remember the shattering sense of shame. My friends in Group 1 wondered, "Who would be next?" I wondered if I would be moved to Group 4 if my inability to do long division continued. Or would it be possible that I could flunk??? The sad reality is, I never learned long division that year anyway.

Tracking and long-term grouping can hurt students in many ways. As Zaslavsky points out, it limits student access to opportunities requiring mathematical competency, tolerates learning climates that discourage achievement, imparts the message that the students are incapable of learning, and allows a situation to continue in which students are bound to lose confidence in their ability to do math.[10] To date, there isn't any evidence that shows that tracking is beneficial for even a majority of students. In fact, the opposite seems to be true. Clearly tracking was created to benefit a few fast or gifted students by removing those students who might impede the progress of others; the plight of the impeders was considered inconsequential. Such a position is wholly out of step with today's commitment to the belief that all students can learn. However, some old practices are hard to kill, even though the research is compelling.

According to Zaslavsky, "In one study of tracking, low-track children were found to challenge their teachers, obstruct academic activity, and misuse educational resources more often than high-track children." Fewer demands were made on low-track students and teachers seemed to be more serious about their high-track students. Low-track children were given more work to do involving isolated skills while high-track children were given more problem-solving opportunities. It seems that when it comes to ability in school, in many cases, "the rich get richer and the poor get worksheets." "Research usually shows no performance decrements for high-ability students in heterogeneous classes, but does show performance decrements for low-ability students in homogeneously grouped classes. Long-term or yearlong groupings, based upon ability within heterogeneous classrooms, produce much the same negative side effects as tracking in homogeneous classrooms. The messages can be just as harmful and long-lasting to students.[11]

Possible Solutions to Problem #3. Collaborative learning strategies that allow children of all abilities to work together in small groups to solve age-appropriate, relevant problems, have proved to be a positive alternative to tracking students as well as a means for significantly increasing student learning. In fact, the research literature on this issue is overwhelmingly powerful and consistent in its message. "Cooperative group work benefits all students, both academically and socially. When students with different abilities, backgrounds, and perspectives explain their thinking and listen to the thinking of others, their reasoning and communication skills are fostered. Additionally, they are exposed to new ideas and strategies, learn to be supportive of and to value others, and become more positive about themselves as learners and more motivated to learn."[12]

Some basic collaborative learning strategies from Dr. Spencer Kagan, known as "Kagan's Co-op Structures"[13] include the following:

Mix-Pair-Discuss. Students pair with classmates to discuss question posed by the teacher.

Numbered Heads Together. Students huddle to make sure all can respond, a number is called, the student with that number responds.

Timed Pair-Share. Students share with a partner for a predetermined amount of time and then the partner shares with them for the same amount of time.

Team Statements. Students think, discuss, write individual statement, Round Robin individual statements, and then work together to make a team statement they can all endorse more strongly than their individual statements.

For more information on Cooperative Learning, please contact Kagan Cooperative Learning, at 1(800) WEE CO-OP.

"You don't have to be a genius to do mathematics. All you need is confidence, persistence, a taste for hard work, and math mental health—the willingness to learn the math you need when you need it."

Sheila Tobias

Do the above strategies imply that one would never work one-on-one with a child with specific needs or perhaps work with several students that need reinforcement or instruction on the same skill? No. There is a huge difference in period skill grouping and tracking. (See the section "Skillshop" in Chapter 8.)

An often overlooked requirement for collaborative work is that the content for collaboration needs to be designed for such work. Having students get together to answer the questions at the end of the chapter or to complete a computation drill is not effective. According to Elizabeth Cohen, the content should be challenging enough so that the highest achieving student in the group cannot do the task by himself or herself. Solving the problem or task requires genuine collaboration to succeed. For more information, see *Designing Groupwork: Strategies for the Heterogeneous Classroom.*[14]

Problem #4: Standardized Testing

Standardized testing is a powerful source of "math anxiety" or "math avoidance." In many classrooms and schools, standardized tests are used as a sole indicator of what a child does or does not know. Such one-shot information often determines placement, tracking and/or long-term grouping, and fuels the Pygmalion effect on teacher expectations.

It is not my intent to either malign or defend standardized tests and their intended purposes versus the reality of their effect. The point here is that standardized testing sends anxiety soaring. Not only do many students quail before these tests, most teachers and administrators also feel a great deal of pressure because they could be, and often are, used as an indicator of their success or failure. To make matters worse, the pressure from the publishing of these scores and fear of the possible consequences for continued funding is also evident. No wonder students aim at "doing well on the test" rather than seeking how to apply math concepts to real world settings. No wonder we adults have concerned ourselves with "teaching to the test" and fear implementing significant change (which invariably is measured and judged prematurely—at the end of the first year of implementation).

I am not implying that these tests are not important. We must be accountable to our children and their families, to our schools and districts, and to ourselves but we must minimize the anxiety and threat they produce.

Possible Solutions to Problem #4. We must stop reinforcing the unintended, negative side effects of assessment in general and standardized tests in particular. We must begin to focus on testing the real thing while realizing that our students will be able to do well on standardized tests by learning mathematical concepts holistically in a way that mirrors math in the real world. By providing children with "being there" experiences they will apply the skills and concepts being learned (see possibilities in Chapter 10) so that a mental program for the desired mathematical performance can be created.

"No other decision that teachers make has greater impact on students' opportunity to learn and on their perceptions about what mathematics is than the selection or creation of the tasks with which the teacher engages the students in studying mathematics. Here the teacher is the architect, the designer of the curriculum."[15]

REALITY CHECK

The purpose of public education is to prepare students to succeed in real life. Thus, the mathematics capabilities that I want to test are the abilities to understand and solve mathematical problems in real life situations and to do so in ways that will allow students to be successful in personal and business finance and in the voting booth. The bottom line is so simple—solving problems for "school math" should be for the sake of solving problems in life! As the saying goes, effective problem-solvers are people who have had a lot of practice solving problems. Begin today to minimize work in textbooks, workbooks, and dittos and start orchestrating opportunities for students to use math to understand the world around them. Base all of your assessment decisions within your classroom on their ability to apply their math understandings. Make an agreement with fellow teachers to use this same information as the source for placement in classrooms from year to year. Use it as the basis for teacher conferences. In short, refuse to misuse standardized test results and insist on focusing on students' ability to apply math concepts in their own lives.

(For easy-to-use structures and procedures for assessing student ability to apply math concepts, the reader may want to refer to *ITI: The Model*, Chapter 9.[16] For more support in providing real-world math experiences for students, see Chapters 9-13 in this book.)

For Further Study

Fear of Math: How To Get Over It and Get On With Your Life
by Claudia Zaslavsky

Humble Pi: The Role Mathematics Should Play in American Education
by Michael K. Smith, Ph.D.

Chapter 3
What Is Math?

So, what is math anyway? Given how many years mathematics has been part of our public school curriculum, it would seem the question should be an easy one to answer, but it is not. Every state and local mathematics organization has its own definitions that change over time with the publication of their newest curriculum guide. I find this very disconcerting. Add to this the reality that what is taught in classrooms across America is primarily arithmetic and one has plenty of reason to be distressed. Why is it so difficult to get consistent, useable answers to the question, "What is math?"

Perhaps what is needed is an everyday, walk-on-the-street, Joe Bag-of-Donuts view. Let's try *Webster's New Collegiate Dictionary:*

> The science of numbers and their operations, interrelations, combinations, generalizations, and abstractions of space configurations and their structure, measurement, transformations, and generalizations.

Although this definition is a mouthful, it is shorter than that found in most math textbooks and yet still maintains the central focus. What leaps off the page is the realization that arithmetic is but a very small aspect of mathematics. Arithmetic alone may have been sufficient for a majority of the population in the horse-and-buggy days but it is woefully insufficient in the 1990s and beyond. This does not mean that children shouldn't have full and complete mastery of arithmetic; they should. . . no question. Arithmetic, the basic skills of math, are a means to an end, just as decoding

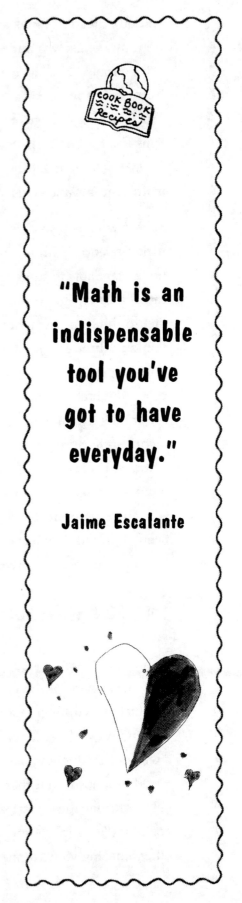

"Math is an indispensable tool you've got to have everyday."

Jaime Escalante

and other reading skills are a means to an end. They are essential but they are not sufficient by themselves and they are not the starting places. Meaningfulness, the desire to solve problems using mathematics, is the beginning and the inner engine that drives learning the basic skills. And meaningfulness is defined by the learner. Real-world math problems are problems the children are experiencing, not the garden variety word problems in a textbook. The focus should be on mathematics in use, for real purposes, not just for taking tests or getting a passing grade. Students must have a reason to need to know math concepts and skills and when and how to apply them.

Yet what is also clear is that mathematics at the elementary grades ought not to be rocket science, with areas and levels of math that are age-inappropriate and thus not understandable to students. To think mathematically does not mean we have to be doing calculus or algebra or thrill to an exploration of prime numbers. For adults in everyday life, to think mathematically includes such things as comparative shopping at a store, thinking through the family (or business) finances, analyzing budget versus expenditures, projecting annual impact of current trends. To think mathematically also includes projecting lifetime costs of one car over another to help make decisions about buying a car or how to make simple carpentry measurements for household repairs, hanging new pictures, etc. Surely preparation for retirement requires the gamut of elementary mathematics skills and knowledge. And so on and so forth. In the spirit of a good home economics course, we could appreciably improve and concretely define a solid mathematics education program for the elementary grades if we analyzed the math applications needed to lead a financially sound adult life, such as home budgets, car and home buying and maintenance, investing in education and training, and planning for retirement.

TOWARD A WORKABLE DEFINITION

For the classroom teacher getting on with his/her day, perhaps the most useful view of "what is math" is to view mathematics as a way of thinking that, according to Howard Gardner, uses different parts of the brain than those used for processing of reading, writing, and music (see Chapter 4 for a discussion of logical-mathematical intelligence). It is a way of thinking with a language of its own, a set of tools for unlocking meaning in the world around us and then communicating that meaning to others. Such a view would help us bridge the typical student perspective of math as "pluses, take aways, times, and gozintas ("goes into") and what teachers often view as the impossible—"new math" and other amazing views of math from the perspective of mathematicians.

It's About Life

Throughout this book and on the front cover echoes the phrase, "It's not about math, it's about life." That is the touchstone of this book and it should be the bedrock of math curriculum. Math is not something you do just in the classroom, as an artifact of getting through the school day. It is a prerequisite for succeeding in day-to-day living in the high tech society of the late 20th and early 21st centuries. Thus, our pictures of what the NCTM standards and literacy goals look like must shift away from the worksheets with talking frogs and dancing bears to scenes of math on the streets, on the job, and in the home—the math being used to accomplish a personal/family need or achieve a goal in the workplace. Worksheets alone cannot produce mathematical literacy; math in the context of real life can.

Pictures of Real Math . . . on the Job. Perhaps the best pictures of mathematics in real life applications come from being "on the job." As adults we have experience with various occupations (as worker or client) and can see how the concepts and skills are used and, in fact, are often central to the performance of that job. Just looking through them begins to stir our sense of what's possible and what is needed as a perspective for answering the question, "What is math?" Math is a lot more than arithmetic and very, very omnipresent in adult life, particularly in the 21st century. Many times, students ask the question, When am I ever going to have to use this?" in reference to a particular skill. Well, Hal Saunders, author of the book, *When Are We Ever Gonna Have To Use This?* beautifully illustrates this to students and teachers. To support you and your students in seeing how math concepts and skills are needed by various occupations, please refer to the chart from Saunders' book starting on the next page. This chart can also be purchased from Books for Educators.

Don't overlook the role of resource people. Schedule a mental math and graphing day and bring in several resource people to take kids through the kinds of mental math they do on an hourly basis. Make it real! Make it purposeful! Make it fun!

What Is Math?

When Are We Ever Gonna Have To Use This? by Hal Saunders

The following chart shows usage of mathematics in 100 occupations. Columns at left fall under the heading **Basic Algebra\Pre Algebra**; columns at right fall under **Algebra Partial Listing**.

Occupation	Fractions	Decimals	Ratio and Proportion	Percent	Customary Measurement	Metric Measurement	Measurement Conversion	Basic Probability	Basic Statistics	Statistical Graphing	Powers and Roots	Other Number Bases	Negative Numbers	Scientific Notation	Basic Problem Solving	Using Formulas	Linear Equations
Accountant (C.P.A.)	●	●	●	●	●			●	●	●			●		●	●	●
Advertising Account Exec.	●	●	●	●	●		●	●	●	●			●		●	●	●
Airline Flight Attendant		●															
Airline Pilot (commercial)			●		●	●	●		●				●		●	●	
Architect	●	●	●	●	●	●	●		●	●	●		●		●	●	●
Assembler (Electronics)	●	●	●	●	●	●	●		●				●		●		
Attorney	●	●	●	●	●			●	●	●	●		●		●	●	
Auto Body Repair Worker	●	●	●	●	●						●				●		
Auto Mechanic		●	●	●	●	●	●				●				●	●	●
Bank Teller		●		●					●				●		●		
Biologist	●	●	●	●	●	●	●		●	●	●	●	●	●	●	●	●
Business Planner	●	●	●	●				●	●	●			●		●	●	●
Cable Splicer	●	●			●		●		●	●		●	●		●		
Cameraperson (TV)	●	●		●	●				●				●		●	●	
Carpenter	●	●		●	●		●								●		●
Ceramic Artist	●	●	●	●	●	●	●	●	●	●					●	●	●
Chef / Caterer	●	●	●	●	●	●	●								●	●	
Chief Exec. Officer (Bank)		●	●	●				●	●	●			●		●	●	
Chief Financial Officer (Bank)		●	●	●		●		●	●	●			●		●	●	
Chiropractor	●	●	●	●	●			●	●				●	●	●	●	
Computer Operator	●	●							●	●		●			●	●	
Comp. Programmer (Business)	●	●	●	●	●		●	●	●	●		●	●	●	●	●	●
Comp. Programmer (Real Time)	●	●	●	●	●	●	●	●	●	●	●	●	●	●	●	●	●
Computer Systems Analyst	●	●	●	●	●	●	●		●	●			●		●	●	●
Computer Technician (Micros)	●	●	●	●	●	●			●	●	●	●	●	●	●	●	●
Cosmetologist		●		●	●										●		
Curator (Art Museum)	●	●	●	●	●	●	●		●	●					●		
Dental Assistant		●		●											●		
Dentist (General)		●	●	●		●	●	●	●				●	●	●		
Dietitian	●	●	●	●	●	●	●		●	●			●		●	●	
Disc Jockey					●												
Disease Registry Technician	●	●	●	●	●		●	●	●	●	●		●	●	●	●	●
Doctor (Internist)	●	●	●	●	●	●	●	●	●	●			●	●	●	●	●
Drafter (Engineering)		●	●	●	●	●	●			●			●	●	●	●	●
Electrician (Residential)	●	●	●	●		●				●					●	●	●
Electronics Technician	●	●	●	●	●		●		●	●	●	●	●	●	●	●	●
(Aerospace) Engineer	●	●	●	●	●	●	●	●	●	●	●	●	●	●	●	●	●
(Air Quality) Engineer	●	●	●	●	●	●	●	●	●	●	●		●	●	●	●	●
(Chemical) Engineer	●	●	●	●	●	●	●		●	●	●		●	●	●	●	●
(Electronics) Engineer	●	●	●	●	●	●			●	●	●	●	●	●	●	●	●
(Mechanical) Engineer	●	●	●	●	●	●	●		●	●	●		●	●	●	●	●
(Microwave) Engineer	●	●	●	●	●	●	●		●	●	●		●	●	●	●	●
(Process) Engineer	●	●	●	●	●	●	●		●	●	●		●	●	●	●	●
(Quality Control) Engineer	●	●	●	●	●	●	●		●	●	●	●	●	●	●	●	●
(Structural) Engineer	●	●	●	●	●		●			●			●	●	●	●	●
Engineering Technician	●	●	●	●	●	●	●		●	●	●		●	●	●	●	●
Farm Operator	●	●	●	●	●		●		●	●			●		●	●	●
Financial Planner (Personal)	●	●	●	●					●	●			●		●	●	
Firefighter	●	●	●	●	●		●		●	●					●	●	
Forest Ecologist	●	●	●	●	●	●	●	●	●	●			●	●	●	●	●

Acknowledgements

Saunders, Hal. Updated Third Edition *When Are We Ever Gonna Have To Use This?* chart showing usage of mathematics in 100 occupations. California: Dale Seymour Publications, 1991. Reprinted by permission of the publisher.

The chart below shows which mathematics topics are used in each occupation. The left group of topics is labeled **Basic Algebra / Pre Algebra** and the right group **Algebra Partial Listing**.

Occupation	Fractions	Decimals	Ratio and Proportion	Percent	Customary Measurement	Metric Measurement	Measurement Conversion	Basic Probability	Basic Statistics	Statistical Graphing	Powers and Roots	Other Number Bases	Negative Numbers	Scientific Notation	Basic Problem Solving	Using Formulas	Linear Equations
Forestry Technician	•	•	•	•	•		•		•	•	•		•		•	•	•
General Contractor	•	•	•	•	•	•	•	•	•	•	•				•	•	•
Golf Pro		•	•	•		•	•	•	•				•		•		
Graphic Artist	•	•		•					•						•		
Highway Patrol Officer		•	•	•		•							•		•		
Homemaker	•	•	•	•	•	•	•		•				•		•	•	
Instrument Tech. (Air Quality)	•	•	•	•	•	•			•	•	•	•	•	•	•	•	•
Insurance Agent		•	•	•					•				•		•	•	
Interior Designer	•	•	•	•		•			•				•		•	•	
International Marketer	•	•	•	•					•	•			•		•		
Landscape Gardener	•	•	•	•					•	•			•		•		
Librarian (Cataloguing)	•	•	•	•			•	•					•		•		•
Machinist (Prototype)	•	•	•	•		•					•	•	•		•	•	•
Market Researcher	•	•	•	•			•	•	•	•	•		•		•	•	•
Medical Lab Technologist	•	•	•	•	•	•			•	•	•	•	•		•	•	•
Medical Researcher	•	•	•	•					•	•			•		•	•	•
Motel Manager		•			•	•			•						•		
Newspaper Reporter	•	•	•	•	•	•	•	•	•				•		•	•	
Nuclear Machine Tech.	•	•	•		•	•	•	•	•	•			•		•	•	•
Nurse	•	•	•	•	•	•	•		•				•		•	•	
Optician	•	•	•	•		•			•	•			•		•		
Optometrist	•	•	•	•	•	•			•		•		•		•	•	•
Painting Contractor	•	•	•	•		•			•	•			•		•	•	
Paralegal	•	•		•									•		•	•	•
Payroll Supervisor	•	•		•											•		
Personnel Manager	•	•	•	•	•		•		•				•		•	•	•
Pharmacist (Community)	•	•	•	•	•	•	•		•	•			•		•	•	•
Photographer (Commercial)	•	•	•		•	•	•			•	•		•		•	•	
Physical Therapist		•	•	•	•	•	•	•	•	•					•	•	•
Physicist (Research)	•	•	•	•	•	•			•		•	•	•	•	•	•	•
Plumber	•	•	•	•	•	•									•	•	•
Printer	•	•	•	•	•		•	•	•						•	•	•
Psychotherapist		•	•	•					•						•		
Public Relations Director	•	•	•	•			•	•	•				•		•		
Real Estate Agent	•	•	•	•			•		•				•		•	•	
Recreation Supervisor		•	•	•			•	•	•				•		•	•	
Restaurant Manager		•	•	•	•			•	•	•			•		•	•	
Retail Sales Person		•	•			•									•		
Road Maintenance Worker		•	•	•	•	•			•						•	•	
Secretary (Administrative)	•	•		•											•		
Small Business Owner	•	•	•	•	•		•		•				•		•	•	•
Stock Broker	•	•	•	•	•	•	•		•				•		•	•	•
Surveyor (Land)		•	•	•	•	•			•		•		•		•	•	•
Travel Agent	•		•	•	•	•			•	•					•	•	
Urban Planner	•	•	•	•	•	•	•		•				•		•	•	•
Veterinarian	•	•	•	•	•	•	•	•	•		•	•	•		•	•	•
Wage / Salary Analyst	•	•	•	•	•				•				•		•	•	•
Waiter / Waitress	•	•	•	•		•			•				•		•		
Welder - Fabricator	•	•	•	•		•			•				•		•		
X-Ray Technician	•	•	•	•	•	•	•	•	•		•	•	•	•	•		

Acknowledgements
Saunders, Hal. Updated Third Edition *When Are We Ever Gonna Have To Use This?* chart showing usage of mathematics in 100 occupations.
California: Dale Seymour Publications, 1991. Reprinted by permission of the publisher.

23

What Is Math?

Occupation	Coordinate Graphing (2-D)	Algebraic Representation	Basic Terminology	Angle Measurement	Pythagorean Theorem	Circles	Area	Volume	Make/Use 3-D Drawings	Calculus and Higher Math	Basic Calculator Use	Scientific Calculator Use	Computer Use	Computer Programming	Group Problem Solving	Mental Math	Induct/Deduct Reasoning	Math Communication	Math Modeling
			Geometry · Partial Listing							Other Topics									
Accountant (C.P.A.)		●					●			●		●			●	●	●		●
Advertising Account Exec.		●	●	●						●		●			●	●	●		
Airline Flight Attendant												●			●	●			
Airline Pilot (commercial)			●	●								●			●	●	●		
Architect			●	●	●	●	●	●	●	●	●	●			●	●		●	●
Assembler (Electronics)			●					●		●		●			●	●			
Attorney			●	●	●		●	●		●		●			●	●			
Auto Body Repair Worker			●	●						●						●			
Auto Mechanic			●	●			●	●		●						●	●		
Bank Teller												●			●	●			
Biologist	●	●	●	●			●	●		●	●	●	●		●	●	●	●	●
Business Planner	●	●								●	●	●			●	●	●	●	●
Cable Splicer			●												●	●			
Cameraperson (TV)			●	●								●			●	●			
Carpenter		●	●	●	●		●	●	●	●						●			
Ceramic Artist		●	●	●			●	●	●	●						●			●
Chef / Caterer				●						●						●			
Chief Exec. Officer (Bank)							●	●	●	●		●			●	●	●		●
Chief Financial Officer (Bank)	●	●	●							●	●	●			●	●	●	●	●
Chiropractor	●		●	●		●		●		●		●			●	●	●		
Computer Operator												●	●	●	●	●	●		
Comp. Programmer (Business)	●	●	●							●		●	●	●	●	●	●	●	●
Comp. Programmer (Real Time)	●	●	●	●	●	●	●	●	●	●	●	●	●	●	●	●	●	●	●
Computer Systems Analyst		●								●		●	●	●	●	●	●	●	●
Computer Technician (Micros)		●					●		●	●		●	●	●	●	●	●	●	
Cosmetologist			●	●											●				
Curator (Art Museum)			●	●	●		●		●	●		●			●	●	●		
Dental Assistant																●			
Dentist (General)	●		●	●				●				●			●	●	●	●	●
Dietitian										●		●			●	●	●	●	
Disc Jockey																●			
Disease Registry Technician	●	●					●	●		●	●				●	●	●	●	●
Doctor (Internist)	●	●	●	●	●		●		●	●	●				●	●	●		
Drafter (Engineering)	●		●	●	●	●		●	●	●	●	●			●	●		●	
Electrician (Residential)		●	●	●	●		●	●	●	●				●	●	●			
Electronics Technician	●	●	●	●	●		●			●	●	●	●		●				●
(Aerospace) Engineer	●	●	●	●	●	●	●		●	●	●	●	●	●	●	●	●	●	●
(Air Quality) Engineer	●	●	●	●	●	●	●	●	●	●	●	●	●	●	●	●	●	●	●
(Chemical) Engineer	●	●	●	●	●	●	●	●		●	●	●	●	●	●	●	●	●	●
(Electronics) Engineer	●	●	●	●	●		●		●	●	●	●	●	●	●	●	●	●	●
(Mechanical) Engineer	●	●	●	●	●	●	●	●	●	●	●	●	●	●	●	●	●	●	●
(Microwave) Engineer	●	●	●	●	●	●	●	●	●	●	●	●	●	●	●	●	●	●	●
(Process) Engineer	●	●	●	●	●		●	●		●	●	●	●	●	●	●	●	●	●
(Quality Control) Engineer	●	●	●	●	●		●			●	●	●	●		●	●	●	●	●
(Structural) Engineer	●	●	●	●	●	●	●	●	●	●	●	●	●		●	●	●	●	●
Engineering Technician	●	●	●	●	●		●			●	●	●	●		●	●	●	●	●
Farm Operator			●		●		●	●	●	●		●			●				
Financial Planner (Personal)										●	●	●			●	●	●		
Firefighter			●	●			●	●		●		●			●	●	●		
Forest Ecologist	●	●	●	●	●		●	●	●	●	●	●			●	●	●	●	●

Acknowledgements

24   Saunders, Hal. Updated Third Edition *When Are We Ever Gonna Have To Use This?* chart showing usage of mathematics in 100 occupations. California: Dale Seymour Publications, 1991. Reprinted by permission of the publisher.

Chart showing usage of mathematics in occupations. Two major column groups: **Geometry · Partial Listing** and **Other Topics**.

Occupation	Coordinate Graphing (2-D)	Algebraic Representation	Basic Terminology	Angle Measurement	Pythagorean Theorem	Circles	Area	Volume	Make/Use 3-D Drawings	Calculus and Higher Math	Basic Calculator Use	Scientific Calculator Use	Computer Use	Computer Programming	Group Problem Solving	Mental Math	Induct./Deduct Reasoning	Math Communication	Math Modeling
Forestry Technician			•	•	•		•	•	•		•		•		•	•			
General Contractor			•	•	•		•	•			•		•		•	•	•		
Golf Pro			•		•			•			•		•		•	•	•		
Graphic Artist			•	•				•			•		•		•	•			
Highway Patrol Officer			•	•		•					•		•		•	•			
Homemaker			•	•			•				•		•		•	•			
Instrument Tech. (Air Quality)	•	•	•	•	•		•	•	•		•	•	•		•	•	•		
Insurance Agent			•				•				•		•		•	•			
Interior Designer			•				•				•		•		•	•			
International Marketer							•	•			•		•		•	•			
Landscape Gardener			•	•		•	•	•			•		•		•	•			
Librarian (Cataloguing)	•			•			•	•			•		•		•	•			
Machinist (Prototype)			•	•	•	•	•	•			•	•	•	•	•	•	•		
Market Researcher	•	•	•				•	•			•	•	•	•	•	•	•	•	
Medical Lab Technologist	•	•	•	•					•		•	•	•		•	•			
Medical Researcher	•	•	•	•				•			•	•	•		•	•	•	•	
Motel Manager							•				•		•		•				
Newspaper Reporter			•	•			•	•			•		•		•	•			
Nuclear Machine Tech.		•	•	•			•		•		•		•		•	•			•
Nurse			•	•			•				•		•		•	•	•		
Optician			•	•					•		•		•		•	•			
Optometrist	•	•	•	•	•	•	•	•	•		•		•		•	•	•	•	
Painting Contractor			•				•				•		•		•	•			
Paralegal		•			•						•		•		•	•	•		
Payroll Supervisor			•								•		•		•				
Personnel Manager			•				•	•			•		•		•	•	•		
Pharmacist (Community)			•								•		•		•				
Photographer (Commercial)			•	•			•		•		•		•		•	•			
Physical Therapist			•	•					•		•		•		•	•	•		
Physicist (Research)	•	•	•	•	•	•	•	•	•	•	•	•	•	•	•	•	•	•	
Plumber			•	•			•	•	•						•	•	•		
Printer			•	•			•	•			•		•		•	•			
Psychotherapist												•			•	•		•	
Public Relations Director			•				•				•		•		•	•	•		
Real Estate Agent			•				•		•		•		•		•	•			
Recreation Supervisor			•	•			•				•		•		•	•	•		
Restaurant Manager			•	•			•	•			•		•		•	•			
Retail Sales Person			•										•		•	•			
Road Maintenance Worker			•				•	•	•				•		•	•			
Secretary (Administrative)											•		•		•				
Small Business Owner		•	•	•			•	•	•		•		•		•	•	•		•
Stock Broker	•	•	•								•		•		•	•	•		•
Surveyor (Land)	•	•	•	•	•	•	•	•	•		•	•	•	•	•			•	
Travel Agent	•		•								•		•		•				
Urban Planner	•	•	•		•		•	•			•		•		•	•		•	
Veterinarian		•	•	•	•	•	•	•			•		•	•	•	•	•		
Wage / Salary Analyst	•	•	•				•				•	•	•	•	•	•	•	•	
Waiter / Waitress											•				•				
Welder - Fabricator			•	•	•		•	•	•		•				•				
X-Ray Technician			•	•			•		•			•		•	•		•		

Acknowledgements
Saunders, Hal. Updated Third Edition *When Are We Ever Gonna Have To Use This?* chart showing usage of mathematics in 100 occupations. California: Dale Seymour Publications, 1991. Reprinted by permission of the publisher.

"Writing about mathematical papers is different from writing about mathematics but I think there needn't, and shouldn't, be such a chasm between the two activities."

John Allen Paulos

Pictures of Real Math . . . in the Home. For pictures of real math in the real world, reachable from the classroom, take a look at Chapter 13, Practical Applications: Math at Home—A Guide to Assist Parents, a chapter intended to show parents how to "find" math experiences at home, as close as the air they breathe. These examples for parents, because they capture real math about the house and home, are also useful for teachers as they help us replace our old pictures of math activities (even those using manipulatives that are representational, not real) with real-life examples that students can fully experience. Use these as examples to jump start your own creative juices.

Making a Professional Commitment

As is true in so many areas of education, the content of mathematics curriculum is a reflection of extremes: in practice, it is primarily arithmetic only; on paper, it is the moon and the calculus to get there. What is needed is a reasonable definition on paper (the written district/school curriculum) and a professional commitment to translate it into action.

Toward a Written Curriculum. The National Council of Teachers of Mathematics (NCTM) provides what it calls "consistent standards." They remind us that math is more than arithmetic and provide an excellent starting place for building a solid, useful mathematics curriculum.

The NCTM "standards" for mathematics[1] for grades K-4 include both process and content.

Process Standards:

1. Mathematics as problem solving, including

    • use problem-solving approaches to investigate and understand mathematical content;

    • formulate problems from everyday and mathematical situations;

- develop and apply strategies to solve a wide variety of problems;

- verify and interpret results with respect to the original problems;

- acquire confidence in using mathematics meaningfully.

2. Mathematics as communication, including

- relate physical materials, pictures, and diagrams to mathematical ideas;

- reflect on and clarify their thinking about mathematical ideas and situations;

- relate their everyday language to mathematical language and symbols;

- realize that representing, discussing, reading, writing, and listening to mathematics are a vital part of learning and using mathematics.

3. Mathematics as reasoning, including

- draw logical conclusions about mathematics;

- use models, known facts, properties, and relationships to explain their thinking;

- justify their answers and solution processes;

- use patterns and relationships to analyze mathematical situations;

- believe that mathematics makes sense.

4. Mathematical connections, including

- link conceptual and procedural knowledge;

- relate various representations of concepts or procedures to one another;

- recognize relationships among different topics in mathematics;

- use mathematics in other curriculum areas;

- use mathematics in their daily lives.

Content Standards:

5. Estimation

- explore estimation strategies;

- recognize when an estimate is appropriate;

- determine the reasonableness of results;

- apply estimation in working with quantities, measurement, computation, and problem solving.

6. Number sense and numeration, including

- construct number meanings through real-world experiences and the use of physical materials;

- understand our numeration system by relating counting, grouping, and place-value concepts;

- develop number sense;

- interpret the multiple uses of numbers encountered in the real world.

7. Concepts of whole number operations, including

- develop meaning for the operations by modeling and discussing a rich variety of problem situations;

- relate the mathematical language and symbolism of operations to problem situations and informal language;

- recognize that a wide variety of problem structures can be represented by a single operation;

- develop operation sense.

8. Whole number computation, including

- model, explain, and develop reasonable proficiency with basic facts and algorithms;

- use a variety of mental computation and estimation techniques;

- use calculators in appropriate computational situations;

- select and use computation techniques appropriate to specific problems and determine whether the results are reasonable.

9. Geometry and spatial sense, including

- describe, model, draw, and classify shapes;

- investigate and predict the results of combining, subdividing, and changing shapes;

- develop spatial sense;

- relate geometric ideas to number and measurement ideas;

- recognize and appreciate geometry in their world.

10. Measurement, including

- understand the attributes of length, capacity, weight, mass, area, volume, time, temperature, and angle;

- develop the process of measuring and concepts related to units of measurement;

- make and use estimates of measurement;

- make and use measurements in problem and everyday situations.

11. Statistics and probability

- collect, organize, and describe data;

- construct, read, and interpret displays of data;

- formulate and solve problems that involve collecting and analyzing data;

- explore concepts of chance.

12. Fractions and decimals

- develop concepts of fractions, mixed numbers, and decimals;

- develop number sense for fractions and decimals;

- use models to relate fractions to decimals and to find equivalent fractions;

- use models to explore operations on fractions and decimals;

- apply fractions and decimals to problem situations.

13. Patterns and relationships

- recognize, describe, extend, and create a wide variety of patterns;

- represent and describe mathematical relationships;

- explore the use of variables and open sentences to express relationships;

The NCTM "standards" for mathematics for grades 5-8 [2] include both process and content.

Process Standards:

1. Mathematics as problem solving

- use problem-solving approaches to investigate and understand mathematical content;

- formulate problems from situations within and outside mathematics;

- develop and apply a variety of strategies to solve problems, with emphasis on multistep and nonroutine problems;

- verify and interpret results with respect to the original problem situation;

- generalize solutions and startegies to new problem situations;

- acquire confidence in using mathematics meaningfully.

2. Mathematics as communication

    *   model situations using oral, written, concerete, pictorial, graphical, and algebraic methods;

    *   reflect on and clarify their own thinking about mathematical ideas and situations;

    *   develop common understandings of mathematical ideas, including the role of definitions;

    *   use the skills of reading, listening, and viewing to interpret and evaluate mathematical ideas;

    *   discuss mathematical ideas and make conjectures and convincing arguments;

    *   appreciate the value of mathematical notation and its role in the development of mathematical ideas.

3. Mathematics as reasoning

    *   recognize and apply deductive and inductive reasoning;

    *   understand and apply reasoning processes, with special attention to spatial reasoning and reasoning with proportions and presentations;

    *   make and evaluate mathematical conjectures and arguments;

    *   validate their own thinking;

    *   appreciate the pervasive use and power of reasoning as a part of mathematics.

4. Mathematical connections

    *   see mathematics as an integrated whole;

    *   explore problems and describe results using graphical, numerical, physical, algebraic, and verbal mathematical models or presentations;

    *   use a mathematical idea to further their understanding of other mathematical ideas;

    *   apply mathematical thinking and modeling to solve problems that arise in other disciplines, such as art, music, psychology, science, and business;

    *   value the role of mathematics in our culture and society.

Content Standards:

5. Number and number relationships

    *   understand, represent, and use numbers in a variety of equivalent forms (integer, fraction, decimal, percent, exponential, and scientific notation) in real-world and mathematical problem situations;

- develop number sense for whole numbers, fractions, decimals, integers, and rational numbers;

- understand and apply ratios, proportions, and percents in a wide variety of situations;

- investigate relationships among fractions, decimals, and percents;

- represent numerical relationships in one-and two-dimensional graphs.

6. Number systems and number theory

- understand and appreciate the need for numbers beyond the whole numbers;

- develop and use order relationships for whole numbers, fractions, decimals, integers and rational numbers;

- extend their understanding of whole number operations to fractions, decimals, integers, and rational numbers;

- understand how the basic arithmetic operations are related to one another;

- develop and apply number theory concepts (e.g., primes, factors, and multiples) in real-world and mathematical problem situations.

7. Computation and estimation

- compute with whole numbers, fractions, decimals, integers, and rational numbers;

- develop, analyze, and explain procedures for computation and techniques for estimation;

- select and use an appropriate method for computing from among mental arithmetic, paper-and-pencil, calculator, and computer methods;

- use computation, estimation, and proportions to solve problems;

- use estimation to check the reasonableness of results.

8. Patterns and functions

- describe, extend, analyze, and create a wide variety of patterns;

- describe and represent relationships with tables, graphs, and rules;

- analyze functional relationships to explain how a change in one quantity results in a change in another;

- use patterns and functions to represent and solve problems.

9. Algebra

    - understand the concepts of variable, expression, and equation;

    - represent situations and number patterns with tables, graphs, verbal rules, and equations and explore the interrelationships of their representations;

    - analyze tables and graphs to identify properties and relationships;

    - develop confidence in solving linear equations using concrete, informal, and formal methods;

    - investigate inequalities and nonlinear equations informally;

    - apply algebraic methods to solve a variety of real-world and mathematical problems.

10. Statistics

    - systematically collect, organize, and describe data;

    - construct, read, and interpret tables, charts, and graphs;

    - make inferences and convincing arguments that are based on data analysis;

    - evaluate arguments that are based on data analysis;

    - develop an appreciation for statistical methods as powerful means for decision making.

11. Probability

    - model situations by devising and carrying out experiments or simulations to determine probabilities;

    - model situations by constructing a sample space to determine probabilities;

    - appreciate the power of using a probability model by comparing experimental results with mathematical expectations;

    - make predictions that are based on experimental or theoretical probabilities;

    - develop an appreciation for the pervasive use of probability in the real world.

12. Geometry

    - identify, describe, compare and classify geometric figures;

    - visualize and represent geometric figures with special attention to developing special sense;

    - explore transformations of geometric figures;

    - represent and solve problems using geometric models;

- understand and apply geometric properties and relationships;

- develop an appreciation of geometry as a means of describing the physical world.

13. Measurement

- extend their understanding of the process of measurements;

- estimate, make, and use measurements to describe to the degree of accuracy required in a particular situation;

- understand the structure and use of systems of measurement;

- extend their understanding of the concepts of perimeter, area, volume, angle measurement, capacity, and weight and mass;

- develop the concepts of rates and other derived and indirect measurements;

- develop formulas and procedures for determining measures to solve problems.

The goals of such study, say the NCTM, should reflect the importance of mathematical literacy which it defines for all students. The goals are:

1. learn to value mathematics

2. become confident in their ability to do mathematics

3. become mathematical problem solvers

4. learn to communicate mathematically

5. learn to reason mathematically

For an expanded discussion, plus illustrative problems, see *Curriculum and Evaluation Standards for School Mathematics* by the National Council of Teachers of Mathematics. It is an invaluable guide when developing schoolwide/districtwide mathematics curriculum.

WHAT MATHEMATICS EDUCATION SHOULD BE

Mathematics education should mirror real life. Children shouldn't be able to tell the difference between "school math" and math at home or on the street. Here are some tips I found useful.

- *Teach skills in context, not in isolation.* Children learn the skills of mathematics, such as double-digit addition, triple-digit subtraction, etc., when these skills are taught in the context of real-life application opportunities. Teachers should teach children the needed skills as the need arises, rather than "marching children in lockstep through a sequenced skills curriculum."

- *Expose children to lots of real-life problem solving.* Use problems that children are experiencing this moment, e.g., how many different kinds of shoes are worn in class today? How many are tennis shoe style? How many different brands of tennis shoes are there? Percentages? Compare to a classroom down the hall. Want "big" numbers? Analyze the entire school. Want really big numbers, calculate the total cost of tennis shoes in the school (at an average cost per pair of a sale price selected from today's newspaper). Such real-world kid problems motivate children to become adept problem solvers and plant the seeds of a lifelong love of math.

- *Accept all methods of problem solving.* The methods of finding solutions to mathematical problems may be different for you than they are for your students. Explore with your students how they got their answers, instead of simply marking the problem wrong. We can learn from the process if we also stay focused on the answer.

- *Allow students to make choices.* Teachers should let students choose how they want to solve problems. Some students may want to use manipulatives, while others may want to draw or act it out. If the context of the assigned problem is of no interest to them, let them use a back drop that is relevant to their experience. For example, if applying an IRS tax rate for the salary of a policeman is of little interest to them, let them select their favorite sports hero as a target for the problem or comparative speed of cheetahs and their own pet dog or cat.

The underlying premise is this: Teaching mathematics must be in context to how children experience mathematics in their real lives. Students must be involved in using math purposefully to meet their own needs. Math education must focus on supporting children's natural development, rather than simply trying to control it by breaking it into small parts to be learned in a programmed sequence portrayed in a textbook.

WHAT MATHEMATICS EDUCATION SHOULD NOT BE

Here are some aspects of traditional math programs to avoid.

- *Teaching skills in isolation or in a strict sequence.* Children learn skills best when their need to know them arises in order to solve what the children see as problems real to them.

- *Relying solely on math textbooks and workbooks.* Math textbooks and workbooks focus on teaching skills in isolation. Most do not provide enough practice of the same concept to go through the two steps of learning:

  1) recognizing and understanding the concepts, and
  2) figuring out how to apply them and then locking them into long-term memory.

  A mere page or two per concept or skill is woefully insufficient. Providing practice of basic skills is crucial to mastery, but only when the practice is in context to what is being studied, in a way that makes sense to the student, after the need arises. Additionally, a majority of "real life" problems in the textbooks are contrived.

- *Timing tests.* It isn't how fast a student can solve a problem that is important; what's important is that he or she can understand and apply math computation and concepts. So, we must stop with the timed tests! They cause real stress for many students and, in terms of brain research findings, are not a defensible instructional strategy.

- *Only using worksheets and "drill and kill."*

- *Only testing subskills.* Passing a test on particular subskills means nothing if the student doesn't know when or how to apply them. Instead, focus on a more holistic assessment, integrating the math skills into application opportunities.

THE BOTTOM LINE

Math is not a subject, it is a process. You only do it in real life if you have a purpose. We must learn to balance basic math skills students need with purpose, meaning, and relevancy. Without this balance, we are abandoning our purpose for teaching mathematics in the first place.

For Further Study

Everybody Counts: A Report to the Nation on the Mathematics Education published by National Research Council

Curriculum and Evaluation Standards for School Mathematics by National Council of Teachers of Mathematics

When Are We Ever Gonna Have To Use This? by Hal Saunders

Chapter 4
Through the Looking Glass:

Mathematics Education from the Perspective of Recent Brain Research

No discussion about mathematics education at the dawn of the 21st century is complete without examining the implications of recent research about how the human brain learns. The findings both surprise and amaze us as well as confirm some of our best intuitions. Particularly startling are the findings about the preschool years. Discoveries such as children being able to add before they can count[1] surely unseat our time-worn beliefs about what is "hard" for children to learn.

Thanks to a phenomenal array of technology, we now know more about the human brain than at any time in human history. Any efforts to rethink math curriculum and/or alter instructional practices must be based on a firm understanding of what current brain research can tell us about how the human brain learns.

IT'S ABOUT THE BRAIN

The following brain research findings are but the tip of the iceberg, yet they provide us with a perspective from which to rethink mathematics education.

Brain Research Finding #1

Perhaps the most startling finding is that by age three children have developed an innate sense of numbers and their operations—addition, subtraction, multiplication, and division.[2] The numbers they use are, however, small

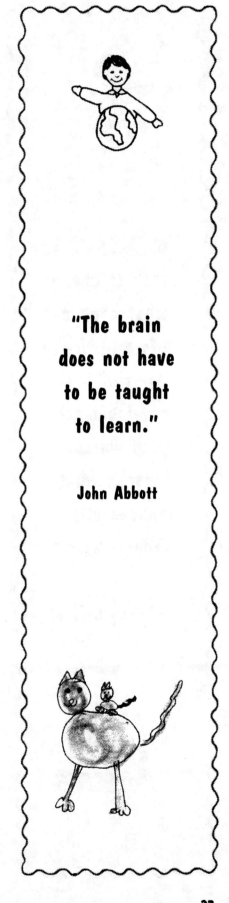

"The brain does not have to be taught to learn."

John Abbott

> "We may not do much to change what happens before birth [in terms of brain development], but we can change what happens after a baby is born."
>
> Dr. Harry Chugani

(typically less than 10). The implications of this one finding are staggering. How we underestimate young children's abilities!

Implications. The biggest lesson here, according to Dr. Robert Wirtz, is "Don't try to teach kids what they already know. It confuses them!" Waiting until third grade to "teach" multiplication and fourth grade to "teach" division is foolishness. Three and four year olds understand division and remainders! If Mom approaches two youngsters with three cookies, they understand the situation: one for each and one remaining.

Teachers in countries such as the Slovak Republic are nonplused: "How can you teach addition without also teaching multiplication? And subtraction without also teaching division?" And while you're teaching division, why not talk about fractions—simple examples, low numbers. Inability to calculate using large numbers is not evidence of inability to understand the concepts of multiplication and division. In Slovakia, children can add, subtract, multiply, and divide by the end of second grade. (And they get there without text books and worksheets; an abacus and real-life items are their only instructional tools.)

Recommended reading. I urge you to do some reading in the area of brain research. My recommendations to you for brain research finding #1 are: *Your Child's Growing Mind: A Practical Guide to Brain Development and Learning from Birth to Adolescence* by Jane M. Healy and *"Anchor" Math* by Leslie Hart.

Brain Research Finding #2

Intelligence is a function of experience. It is the result of physiological growth in the brain, growth which is stimulated by sensory input through the 19 senses. Yes, I said 19, not 5! According to brain research, we have at least 19 senses and the more senses involved when learning, the greater the input to the brain; the greater the input, the greater the physiological change in the brain; the greater the physiological change, the greater the learning and memory retention. As teachers, our challenge is orchestrating experiences that provide the greatest sensory input. For example, consider the following paragraph:

"*Cayard* forced *America* to the left, filling its sails with 'dirty air,' then tacked into a right-hand shift . . . . That proved to be the wrong side. *America*, flying its carbon fiber/liquid crystal main and headsails, found more pressure on the left. *Cayard* did not initiate a tacking duel until *Il Moro* got headed nearly a mile down the leg. *Cayard* did not initiate a jibing duel to improve his position heading downwind and instead opted for a more straight-line approach to the finish."[3]

Questions? Yes, we assume this paragraph has something to do with sailing and we could answer questions such as these:

- How far ahead did *Il Moro* get before *Cayard* initiated a jibing duel?

- What kind of air filled *America's* sails?

But, what do we really understand? If we've sailed before, probably quite a bit. If we've never been on or near a sailboat, probably not much. Likewise, how much do students understand about percentages? Unless they've been paid on commission or figured the profit margin for their business, probably not much. If students come to us without the needed real world experience to understand the math concepts we wish to teach them, then we must orchestrate experiences that will provide maximum sensory input.

The 19 senses are:[4]

SENSES	KIND OF INPUT
Sight	Visible light
Hearing	Vibrations in the air
Touch	Tactile contact
Taste	Chemical molecular
Smell	Olfactory molecular
Balance	Kinesthetic geotropic
Vestibular	Repetitious movement
Temperature	Molecular motion
Pain	Nociception
Eidetic imagery	Neuroelectrical image retention
Magnetic	Ferromagnetic orientation
Infrared	Long electromagnetic waves
Ultraviolet	Short electromagnetic waves
Ionic	Airborne ionic charge
Vomeronasal	Pheromonic sensing
Proximal	Physical closeness
Electrical	Surface charge
Barometric	Atmospheric pressure
Geogravimetric	Sensing mass differences

Six kinds of input are:[5]

For an illustration[6] of which senses are activated by each of these kinds of input, see pages 4.8 and 4.9.

Using the Cayard sailing example for a moment, and the powerful sensory input that occurs during "being there" experiences, consider how many countless thousands of uneducated sailors successfully learned about coordinates, longitude and latitude, geometry (use of angles to determine position), measurement, velocity, inertia, and much more, because of the vast sensory input from "being there" experiences as compared to the paltry percentage of students who learn these concepts, at the level of application, from textbook and lecture (with their minimal sensory input).

The key idea here is that, when we move beyond arithmetic to mathematical concepts, we must ensure that we provide students "being there" experiences where those math concepts are needed and being used.

Clearly "being there," immersion, and hands-on opportunities provide significantly more sensory input than that of traditional instruction. Textbooks and workbooks elicit only two or three of the 19 senses; manipulatives add only one more.

Implications. Children should learn to "see" math in their everyday lives and to "talk" about it as it is relevant and meaningful to them. Division and fractions come up at every meal. For example, four cookies and three children are an obvious invitation to discuss division (and remainders!) and pizza is a natural happening to prompt a discussion of fractions. Susan Kovalik's four-year old niece arrived at the fundamental understanding that "the larger the number of pieces, the smaller each piece" without prompting. Precocious? Her aunt thinks so! But such ahha's are not unusual when children are given the opportunity to "experience" the numbers and are invited to explore the world through quantification.

What children need from kindergarten and upward is lots of real life experience, including experiences with what Leslie Hart calls "N-ness," a sense of numbers, the quantity that each number represents. For example, what is a dozen; about how much is five gallons of water; is this pile of pennies about a dollar's worth? Experience with real world things in real world situations develops spatial abilities and an inner picture of what the numbers are doing, making estimation easy and accurate (knowing if the estimate is within the ball-park) and knowing what operations are needed because of the relationships that need to be calculated. (For more information about developing "N-ness," see *"Anchor" Math* by Leslie Hart.) Once numbers "mean" something to students, they begin to beg for "big" numbers because they can then "see" what those big numbers might mean.

The power of "being there," real life experiences for students should not be underestimated. When Walter E. Jacobson Elementary School in Las Vegas, Nevada, initiated a full-blown, schoolwide microsociety in which every classroom (and many individual students) operated a business throughout the year, standardized math test scores jumped 25 percentile points in one year; the percent of students in the bottom quarter fell by 50% and the percent of students in the top quarter increased by 67%. (For a description of Jacobsonville, see Chapter 11.)

The most powerful message from brain research is this: math must be experienced firsthand, based on *being there* experiences because conceptual development is based on sensory input.

BEING THERE EXPERIENCE ➡ CONCEPT ➡ LANGUAGE ➡ APPLICATION TO REAL WORLD [7]

"Talking about" math works only with those students who have had prior experience with what is being talked about. Conceptual learning occurs when high levels of sensory input from "being there" experiences are processed by the pattern-seeking brain to identify and construct meaning (the concept is understood through the action/events of the location). Language (the attachment of a word to this new understanding) then makes possible further exploration and application (program building for long-term retention and use). The brain readily learns (makes meaning) and applies a mental program for using) the information or skill learned in this sequence.

In marked contrast, conventional schooling starts with language (the introduction of vocabulary words and their definitions) *about* things and attempts to move to concept development. Long-term results are disappointing.

???

LANGUAGE   ● ● ●   CONCEPT   ●   APPLICATION[8]

In her book, *Endangered Minds: Why Our Children Don't Think*, Dr. Jane Healy states that "Without experiences, there are no concepts; without concepts, there's no attention span because they (children) don't know what people are talking about."[9] Without a conceptual understanding of the words, children will not be able to get a picture in their minds about what is happening. "Until then, there is no way they can really understand what kind of an equation is needed."[10] Only when students have engaged in a "being there" experience and have first hand knowledge about how mathematical concepts are at work can we implement numerous teaching strategies to help students become more comfortable with the "math language." As Leslie Hart points out, "provide a lot-a lot- a lot of real world experience."[11] We can begin by applying the same strategies to math that we do to an integrated, holistic, language arts program by writing, reading, speaking, and listening, about mathematical concepts, but only AFTER students have engaged in the real life experience. "The principles underlying language across the curriculum in schools emphasize the necessary link between language and thought, build on the prior experiences all pupils bring to school, and acknowledge the learners' intentions to make sense of new information, including subject matter concepts."[12]

Recommended reading for brain research finding #2: *Inside the Brain* by Ronald Kotulak and "How a Child's Brain Develops: And What It Means for Child Care and Welfare Reform," *Time Magazine*, February 3, 1997. See also *ITI: The Model* (Chapters 3 and 6) and *Kid's Eye View of Science: A Teacher's Handbook for Implementing a Brain-Compatible Approach to Teaching Science, K-6* (Chapters 1 and 5), both by Susan Kovalik & Karen Olsen.

Brain Research Finding #3

Using mathematics to solve a problem or produce a product is a way of thinking that differs from what occurs in the brain when reading literature or history or when playing music or creating art. According to Howard Gardner, processing of high level math problems causes the brain to fire in both left and right hemispheres in the front and in the back. Gardner defines intelligence as a "problem-solving and/or product-producing capability."[13]

Logical-mathematical intelligence is the home of science and math. The core function of this intelligence is the interaction with the world of objects—ordering and reordering them, assessing their quantity, comprehending numerical symbols, appreciating the meaning of signs referring to numerical operations, and understanding the underlying quantities and operations themselves.[14]

This intelligence appears early and the most productive work is done by age forty if not by age thirty. The basis for all logical-mathematical forms of intelligence springs from the handling of objects; later things become internalized ("done in one's head"). One proceeds from objects to statements, from actions to the relations among actions, from the realm of the sensory-motor to the realm of pure abstraction—ultimately to the heights of logic and science.

The good news is that all children have the innate capacity for mathematics; the challenge is that not all have had the support and the mediation necessary to develop it fully by the time they arrive at school. The solution to any perceived deficit is lots of real world input (as defined above) and lots of mediation.[15]

Implications. While it may seem self-evident, it bears underscoring: "doing" mathematics requires development of that part of the brain that processes mathematics and there are no shortcuts! Using the part of the brain that handles linguistics to talk about math does not necessarily spill over into an understanding of math (on the other hand, once understanding is reached, talking about how to use the math concept to solve a here-and-now problem helps cement the understanding into longterm memory).

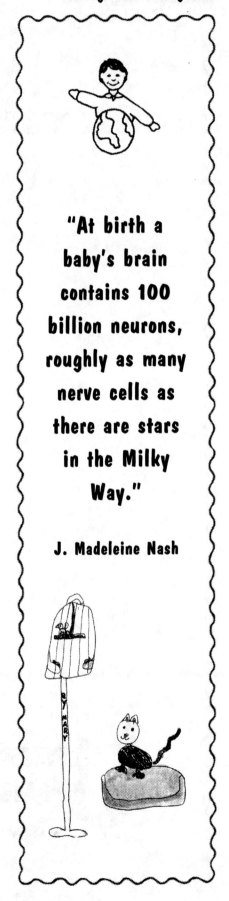

"At birth a baby's brain contains 100 billion neurons, roughly as many nerve cells as there are stars in the Milky Way."

J. Madeleine Nash

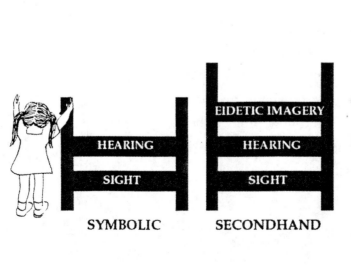

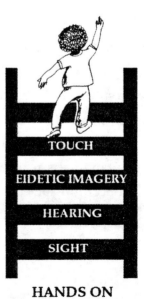

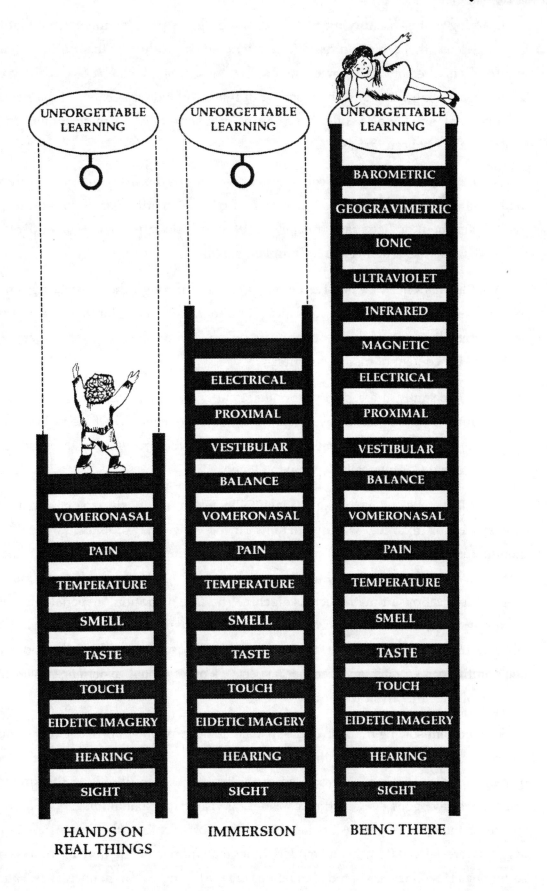

HANDS ON
REAL THINGS

IMMERSION

BEING THERE

Learning math—identifying and understanding the patterns inherent in math and learning to use them to solve real-life problems—is a product of that part of the brain that thinks mathematically. However, once math is learned, it can be talked about using language arts skills. In short, the teaching of math is the development of mathematical intelligence; language arts skills are a means of communicating math understandings that have already been learned.

The critical question for teachers here is: When you teach math, are you thinking mathematically yourself—are you processing from the "math" part of your brain or are you talking about or "language artsing" about math. You must model for students how to use mathematical intelligence for problem-solving.

What learners need is massive amounts of input through the sensory system with wide ranges of real-life experiences calling for quantification, exploration of the patterns and interrelationships of those quantifications, and communicating about them. These should be the content of math education.

Very importantly, the capacity to understand answers resulting from calculation of large numbers, estimation, measurement, geometry, concepts of whole number operations and so forth, often requires the ability to "see" the process and the product—an intelligence that Gardner calls "spatial intelligence."

The initial steps in developing spatial intelligence in relationship to math comes from extensive exposure to real-world situations during which the students first identify and then understand the patterns of mathematics around them. Such experiences with real-world math problems and products provide the building blocks for stepping into more abstract applications of math such as algebra. The core operation of spatial intelligence, according to Gardner, depends on the ability to image. It also involves the capacity to perceive the visual world accurately, perform transformations and modifications upon one's initial perceptions, and recreate aspects of one's visual experience, even in the absence of relevant physical stimuli.

The problem-solving function of the spatial intelligence is the processing of information received, not just the avenue for bringing in information. Spatial intelligence is a collection of related skills. The images produced in the brain are helpful aids to thinking; some researchers have gone even further, considering visual and spatial imagery as a primary source of thought. For many of the world's famous scientists, their most fundamental insights were derived from spatial models rather than from mathematical lines of reasoning. As Stephen Hawkings has noted, "Equations are the boring part of mathematics. I attempt to see things in terms of geometry."[16]

And, as Howard Gardner points out, each of these intelligences operates from a different part of the brain. "Talking" about math (using linguistic intelligence) does not produce math understanding but rather allows one to share what one already understands with others. The ability to communicate about math comes from the ability to think mathematically first, "seeing" the problem and its plausible solutions using spatial intelligence. Once the ability to image a situation or problem in the mind's eye exists, then can we communicate about math linguistically.

While such a conversation about how the brain "thinks" math may seem strange at first, it is a crucial understanding to reach if you truly want to break out of old pictures of arithmetic curriculum and instruction. Even a rudimentary understanding of Gardner's theory of multiple intelligences makes it clear that math is a way of thinking and it requires the ability to image problems and possible solutions. "Talking about" math is a by-product of mathematical understanding not a means to it.

Recommended reading for brain research findings #3: *Seven Kinds of Smart* and *Assessing Multiple Intelligences in the Classroom* by Thomas Armstrong. Source work: *Frames of Mind: The Theory of Multiple Intelligences* by Howard Gardner.

Brain Research Finding #4

Learning is a two step enterprise. First comes identifying and understanding meaningful patterns; second, developing the mental programs for using what is understood—not just once on a test but reliably in similar but varying circumstances in real life contexts.

Pattern-seeking. What is a pattern? Every noun and verb in our personal vocabulary is a pattern, a collection of recognizable attributes important enough to us to have a word assigned to it. For example, the attributes of a cat are a roundish head, svelte body mounted on four legs, paws with retractable claws, a slim, whip-like tail, and a meow sound. Are there other animals with such attributes? Yes, some but not all; a cheetah, for example, has non-retractable claws. Similarly, skipping is a step-hop, step-hop, step-hop gait by a two-legged animal during which only one foot at a time touches the ground.

In the world of math, 1/4, .25, 25%, square root of .0625 are all different patterns for the same quantity. For students with a sense of number-ness, such a statement "makes sense." For those without a sense of number-ness, the response is most likely, "Teacher, you've got to be kidding!" In the world of math, division is merely a short cut to finding out how many cookies each of the four of us will get from a batch of a dozen and a half cookies (and what do we do about the remainder of 2!). Multiplication is merely a fast way to add up numbers.

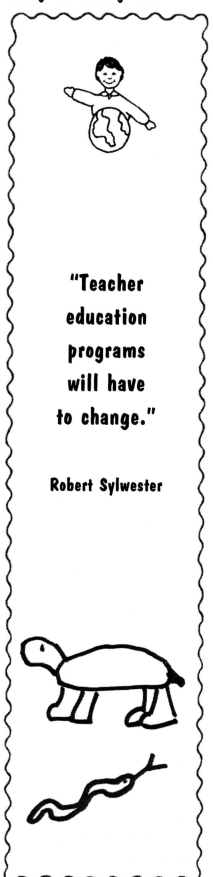

"Teacher
education
programs
will have
to change."

Robert Sylwester

There is a world of difference between teaching by repetition and teaching that points out the attributes of the pattern to be recognized and understood. Rote learning is useful for memorizing things that have no rhyme or reason, such as the order of the alphabet. But rote learning is a very inefficient and often counterproductive way to learn something that has meaningful patterns to it. For example, rote memory of the multiplication tables to 12 requires memorizing 144 combinations. But understanding the pattern of multiplication, i.e., that it is simply a way to chunk numbers together for fast addition, means that I only have to "memorize" those chunkings that take me a couple of seconds to reconstruct in my head or, even more laboriously, on paper. For example, I'm used to putting two or three dozens together because that's the realm of cookie baking and donut buying. But when I get to eight or nine dozen, I resort to memorization. For as Hart comments, "rote memory is always mastered more quickly when understanding is present."[17] As a rule of thumb: memory based upon multiple experiences is always more reliable and useful than memory based solely upon rote repetition.

To summarize the first step in learning: pattern seeking begins with recognizing the attributes of the pattern and ends with constructing an understanding of what the pattern means, does, is, etc.

Developing Programs. The second step in learning is developing a mental program for using what is understood. The initial stage of this step involves figuring out how to use the information or skill in real-life settings (work, recreation, personal life). This stage requires careful monitoring by the teacher (Madeline Hunter's term, "guided practice"), or by students in collaborative learning groups, to ensure that the program being developed is accurate. It is critical to prevent practice of incorrect understandings, something that occurs frequently when students take home a page full of division problems to practice on, for example.

In the realm of mental program building, getting the right answers on the worksheet following direct instruction or getting a 100% on this week's pop quiz is just the beginning. The most important question is whether or not the learning has been wired into long-term memory. Program building takes time and requires multiple opportunities to apply the understanding in real life circumstances (within the child's world as well as adult applications) and to reflect and communicate what is being done in one's own words. Program building is the result of physiological change and growth in the brain—neurons creating connections with other neurons through their dendrites and axons—and practicing those connections until mylenization occurs, a process that cements those connections, so to speak, for future use.

The last stage of developing mental programs, the result of much practice in varying situations in real life, is the expert's ability to perform with practiced ease. As Hart explains, once developed, programs are a complete set of actions to achieve an intended goal, the needed behaviors becoming somewhat automatic. To reiterate, the building of mental programs requires lots of practice with solving, within real world contexts, real problems that are meaningful to kids.

Implications of pattern-seeking and program-building. An understanding of learning as a two-step process fundamentally changes how we view curriculum. Curriculum should be conceptual in nature so that patterns are more easily perceivable (factoids are difficult for children because they are so small an idea, with so few attributes, that pattern detection is difficult and meaningfulness is lost). Also, because concepts are transferable to other situations, which factoids are not, they invite additional practice in using the content which increases the likelihood that the learning will be hard-wired into longterm memory.

Instructional strategies also need to be rethought, particularly in regard to time— adequate time. When we ask students to "put away their math book, it's time for____(the next subject)," we interrupt learning by interrupting the physiological processes in the brain by which it "wires" new learnings into long-term memory.

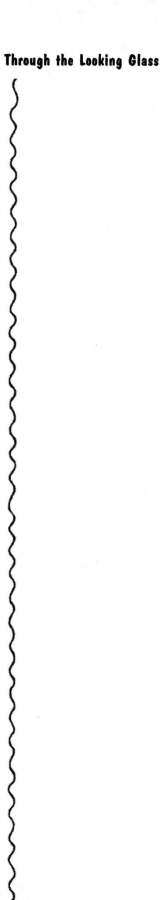

Chapter 5
Language and Mathematics:

Giving Voice to Math Understandings

"Learning does not come from one source,
nor is it best learned from behind a desk,
hands folded, feet flat on the floor, and eyes front.

Before the child entered school,
he learned language actively,
by interacting with his environment.
He used language purposefully to get things done.

As educators, we must go back to the roots of his learning,
to use language to get things done.
We must merge our traditional sense of schooling with
the real world.

What we do in school must not insult the child's past
but must build upon his past and encourage future learning."
—Sigmund A. Boloz, 1985

The first time I encountered this poem by Sigmund A. Boloz, I related it to the work I was doing in my classroom in regards to my integrated language arts program. I felt so connected to this poem that each year I shared it with the parents of my students and hung it up in my classroom. (Several years later, I was doing a training on the Navajo Reservation in Arizona and was introduced to the principal of the school, Sigmund A. Boloz! WOW!)

"For the child in the primary grades, the language of math is best learned when it is integrated into their other studies and informal experiences."

Joanne Oppenheim

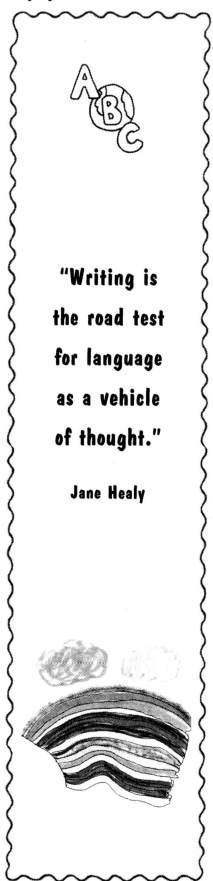

"Writing is
the road test
for language
as a vehicle
of thought."

Jane Healy

I had come a long way in my teaching of language arts. No longer did my students use "English workbooks," English basals, or dittos. Now my students were engaging in REAL writing, reading, listening, and speaking opportunities while being immersed in quality literature on a daily basis.

What I didn't realize at this time, however, was the importance of using *real* language arts strategies to support my teaching of mathematics. For years, I had separated the two subjects as though they never mixed. Now, I can't imagine ever teaching math any other way! Dr. Jane Healy points out that I was not the only educator lacking this connection, "Most people, even math teachers, are not aware that problems with language can cause difficulties in mathematical reasoning. The verbal tools that clarify relationships in reading and writing do the same job in math, and studies of children with exceptional mathematical talents often reveal similarly high verbal skills."[1] How many times have we misunderstood a student having trouble with mathematical concepts, when in reality, the student's difficulty was not at all with the math concepts, but within the comprehension of the language that was asking the question.

If all of the teachers of America were surveyed, and asked, "What do your students have the most difficulty with in math?", I would bet that the majority of them would answer: Story Problems. I can remember my own experiences and frustrations as a child trying to figure out which operation to do to solve a particular story problem. I vividly recall asking my sixth grade teacher, "If you would just tell me if I'm supposed to add, subtract, multiply, or divide, then I can solve the problem." Obviously, I was missing the point. *My point,* however, is that I'm sure I wasn't alone in my thinking, nor do I believe this scenario has vanished from our schools. It was obvious that I didn't have the conceptual understanding of the mathematical language that was asking me the question (and remember,

I was an excellent reader!). The other side of the coin is this, "a student may have the skills necessary to solve a math problem, but lack the reading skills necessary to understand it. A recently arrived foreign born child might not have the cultural references to understand the story."[2]

We think of mathematics as being a logical-mathematical intelligence, requiring a 'good number sense' and comprehensive computational abilities. But math is about communication. In order to be an effective communicator, one must first understand and feel comfortable with the language they are to be engaging in. Math in this country is presented in a verbal-linguistic fashion. The communication that takes place must be *about* something. Is this about semantics? Yes! "Semantics is usually defined as 'the study of meanings." Now, whatever interests people means something to them, so *everything* that interests people-including mathematics-has semantic aspects."[3]

"Math is a language. Like other languages, it uses symbols to communicate ideas. In our spoken language, symbols represent graphemes, which in turn, form morphemes and words. Rules, referred to as grammar, dictate how we organize the symbols into sentences to convey ideas and build concepts."[4] To make sense of any language, we must engage in experiences that help us construct the connection between words and their meanings. MacNeal refers to this as *mathsemantics*. In his book, *Mathsemantics: Making Numbers Talk Sense*, MacNeal, points out how unnatural this may be for young children. "There's no way for the child to construct the needed mathsemantics from ordinary childhood semantics. Numbers (one, two three,. . .) aren't 'things' in the sense the child knows. Names like 'plus,' 'minus,' and 'equals' don't reside in objects. 'Two plus three make five' isn't an arbitrary rule like 'No more talking once the lights are out.' There are more such seeming rules than anyone could possibly remember."[5]

Jane Healy agrees. She states that, "Some words important in beginning math are those that tell about the direction in which the numbers and the thinking go: (e.g., *before, after, into, above, under, away, over*); causation (e.g., *if, then, because*); or actions (e.g., *add, multiply*). The terms borrowing from, dividing into, or multiplying by are only a few examples that often confuse children who have trouble attaching the sequence of the language meaning to the numerals on the page. Advanced math courses such as algebra demand special skills in logical, sequential reasoning that often come wrapped in a form of syntax."[6] Still, it is simply not enough to know *how* to add, subtract, multiply, and divide. "Children also need to know what it means to do those operations and when to do them."[7] "The development of a student's power to use mathematics involves learning the signs, symbols, and terms of mathematics. This is best accomplished in problem situations in which students have an opportunity to read, write, and discuss ideas in which the use of the language of mathematics becomes natural. As students communicate their ideas, they learn to clarify, refine, and consolidate their thinking."[8]

In his book, *Anchor Math*, Leslie Hart points out that there are three levels of math language: "First, 'practical' math, which helps us deal with the mostly concrete world of here and now, including all of our daily transactions, ordering, physical work, current data, etc. Examples: spent $144.75 for clothes, poured 12 cubic yards of concrete, produced 12,000 widgets, have 322 patients in the hospital.

Second, we have 'projective' math, dealing with what should, or could, or might happen. You plan out a trip; or work out estimates for a new business; or figure out how fast a rocket will likely be traveling within four minutes after launch; or how many cases of measles could occur within the next two years.

Third, we have 'investigative' math, where we are interested in trends and relationships, limits, interactions, and, in general, digging out significant concepts by using mathematical techniques. We might analyze election results to see the role played by racial concerns or gain some insight into an intricate chemical reaction. Included would be 'game' math, essentially playing with numbers or mathematical elements for no immediate, 'real' purpose." Hart suggests that these "levels" are offered only to suggest the scope of math language. Elementary school math could be at any of the three levels. "Our purpose, or need, would determine which kind of math we do. Outside of classrooms, nobody does math without some purpose in mind. (That should make us think about some things we do in classrooms.)"[9]

"Communication in mathematics has become important as we move into an era of a 'thinking' curriculum. Students are urged to discuss ideas with each other, to ask questions, to diagram and graph problem situations for clarity . Writing in mathematics classes, once rare, will now be vital."[10] Jane Healy agrees, "Having students write about problems helps them with the kind of logical thinking they need to come up with good solutions. Improving their language skills is her first step in improving mathematical reasoning."[11] So, once students are given the opportunity to engage in 'being there' experiences (see chapter 10), what do these strategies look like when we return to the classroom?

I caution you not to turn your math program into "the *language artsing* of math!" Language arts strategies should only come into practice AFTER students have engaged in experiences which illustrate the purpose of that math concept/skill and provide students a need to know. Then, and only then, should language arts and math strategies be brought together. Marilyn Burns, creator of *Math Solutions* and the author of numerous books for teachers and children, has identified nine ways to incorporate math and writing strategies and are listed below:

1. Talk with students about the purpose of their writing. Make sure students understand the two basic reasons for writing in math class, to enhance and support their learning and to help you assess their progress.

2. Establish yourself as the audience. Explain to students how their writing helps you. Tell them, "What you write shows me what you're learning and what you understand. It helps me think about how to better teach you." During class it's hard to listen to all students describe their thinking, so point out that their writing should include as much detail as possible.

3. Use students' writing in classroom instruction. Children's papers are effective springboards for class discussions and activities. Using them in this way reinforces to the students that you value their writing. Hearing others' ideas shows children different ways to approach problems. Ask children to read their papers aloud. For example, when I asked fifth graders to trace one of their feet on centimeter-squared graph paper, figure out its area, and then describe the process they used, Nelson wrote that he had counted whole squares, added up partial squares that equaled whole ones, and used these numbers to calculate the area. Amy wrote that she had drawn a rectangle around the outline she'd traced and found its area. By listening to what others wrote, students learned about different methods they could have used. This inspired a few to revise their work.

4. Have students discuss their ideas before writing them. For most children, talking is easier than writing, and class discussions allow students to express their ideas and hear others. After a discussion, remind children that they may write about any idea they heard, as long as it makes sense to them and they can explain it.

5. Provide prompts. To help students get started writing, put a prompt on the board, such as, "I think the answer is ___. I think this because _____." (Don't demand that students use the prompts. What's important is that their writing, no matter how they express it, relates to the problem and makes sense).

6. Give individual help to students who don't know what to write. First, talk to students to make sure they understand the assignment. Then try additional prompts, such as: "What do you think?", "What idea do you have?", or "What do you remember about what others said?" Once children offer ideas suggest that they repeat them in their heads before writing them down. I add: "Let the words go from your brain past your mouth, through your shoulder, down your arm, and out through your pencil onto your paper." It's graphic and it works!

7. Post math word lists. Post a list of the different areas of math you're studying-numbers, geometry, measurement, probability, and so on. Then start a word list that directly relates to each. Encourage students to consult the charts for vocabulary and spelling.

8. Ask students to revise and edit. If possible, when children hand in their papers, have them read their work aloud to you. Whenever their papers do not give complete or detailed information-which I find happens more often than not-ask students to revise. You might say, "That's a good beginning" and then give guidance by adding: "Write some more about why you're sure that's correct" or "Give some details or examples to help me better understand your idea."

Depending on the child and the assignment, you might ask a student to make spelling and grammatical corrections. My policy is that students should underline words they don't think they've spelled correctly. Because the purpose of their writing is to give me insights into their understanding-not to be published-sometimes I ask children to correct it and other times I don't. Making a decision in each case is part of the craft of teaching.

9. Read students' work to evaluate your teaching and to assess your progress. Reading class sets of assignments gives you an overview of how the class responded to particular lessons and helps you evaluate the effectiveness of your instructional choices. It also gives you information on each child's understanding.

File student's papers in their individual folders. Keep the papers in order so you'll have a chronological set of work. Reading individual student work done over time gives you a sense of the child's progress."[12] By increasing the amount and purpose of writing in regards to mathematics, we will increase the capacity for our students to understand the language of mathematics.

Math journals are another way to expand on the students' understanding of math as a language. In the chapter entitled, Daily Math Opportunities, I list the use of math journals as a way to help students develop ideas, expand on concepts, and to solve problems. The following menu of ideas, from Sonia Helton, suggest some writing prompts for the use of math journals:

- Explain in your own words the meaning of. . .
- Explain what is most important to understand about.
- Write a letter to a classmate who could not attend class today so that she will understand what we did and learn as much as you did. Be as complete as possible.
- Describe any places you became stuck and how you became unstuck when solving the problem.
- What I like most or least about math
- The most important thing I learned in math this week (or today) is. . .
- If math could be a sound (or shape, or animal), it would be . . .because. . .
- Draw a picture or build a model to illustrate . . .
- How do you know your solution is correct?
- What was the most difficult (or easiest) part of. . .?
- Describe any patterns or parts that are alike in the investigation.
- Write a short plan for what you will do tomorrow on your project.
- Poetry written by the children expressing their feelings about math.
- Math observations (around room, around home, etc. give examples)
- Drawings, illustrations depicting measurement, graphing, charts, estimations, time lines, gathering data, analyzing data, examples of symmetry

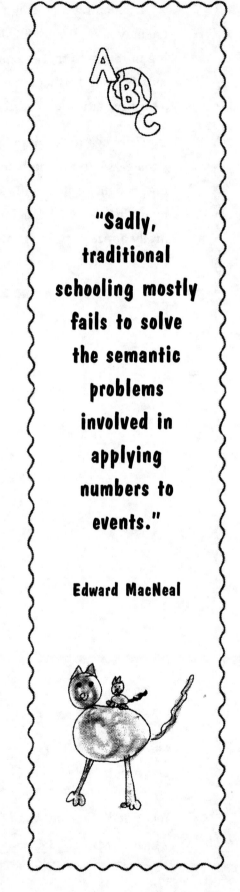

"Sadly, traditional schooling mostly fails to solve the semantic problems involved in applying numbers to events."

Edward MacNeal

Depending on the age and developmental stage of the student, entries into the journal may vary greatly. "Kindergarten students may draw pictures of sets of things, assigning numbers to that set, and then using their numbered pictures to write stories.(Sets of objects could be theme related.) Overall, math journals help build self-esteem as well as a positive attitude toward math."[13]

Once again, the language of math is not simply about the integration of language arts strategies into the math curriculum. It's much bigger than that. We must reflect on giving students opportunities to engage in real life experiences so that they can see how math fits into what is being studied and where the language of those math concepts naturally appear, applying language to the experience *as* it is being experienced.

Remember, it's not about math; it's about life!

For Further Study

Endangered Minds: Why Children Don't Think and What We Can Do About It by Jane M. Healy

Your Child's Growing Mind by Jane M. Healy

"Anchor" Math by Leslie A. Hart

Chapter 6
Math and Technology

Life at the brink of the 21st century is technology-driven. One can no longer go to the bank, the grocery store, or even make a phone call without interacting with the latest technology. While such technologies are becoming increasingly user-friendly, they are not math-less—either in the process of using or in their effects upon our day-to-day lives. Increasingly, math and technology are inseparably linked and therefore to be mathematically literate can no longer be considered the domain only of the "fast-track" elite population of students. To the contrary, "each individual must be equipped with a combination of personal skills, technological skills, and thinking skills in order to apply mathematics meaningfully. These are the prerequisites for understanding the world in which we live, for realizing the potential of technology, and for maintaining our system of government."[1] Thus, it is crucial to provide the tools of technology to our students, enabling them to seek, access, construct, organize, and communicate information in this rapidly changing time.

When we talk about technology, are we all speaking the same language? Many educators think of technology as being limited to calculators and computers. *Webster* defines technology as being "a technical method of achieving a practical purpose." Technical methods include software and models of thinking as well as hardware such as the ubiquitous typewriter, telephone (yes, in the classroom!), telescope, overhead projector, electronics, robotics, and more. "Technologies have always emerged out of our body/brain's limitations. . ." We therefore developed technologies that allow us to do things that are biologically impossible, or that we can do only with great effort.

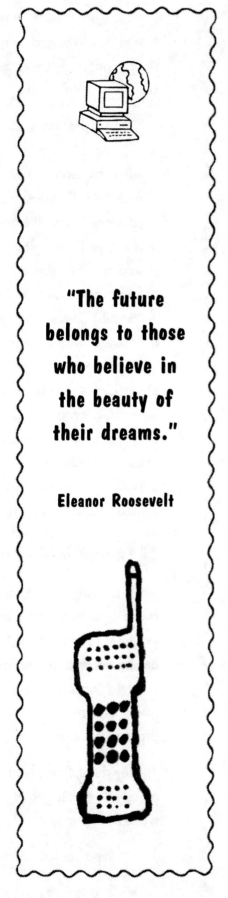

"The future belongs to those who believe in the beauty of their dreams."

Eleanor Roosevelt

Technologies have narrowed the distance between what we can do and what we would like to do."[2] The way any one individual uses technology depends greatly on one's attitude about how to use technology to help us solve our problems. Technology itself is not the problem solver, it is only a medium, another tool for our teacher tool bag, if you will.

In his latest book, *A Celebration of Neurons,* Dr. Robert Sylwester states that, "Schools should not be trying to force students to match the computer's skill in performing some of the more tedious tasks involved in mathematics, written language, and the organization of data. This doesn't mean that we shouldn't continue to teach arithmetic computation, for example. It's easier to master such basic facts as 3 x 4 in our mind than it is to depend on a calculator. On the other hand, for a problem such as 345 x 56, which we would traditionally compute with paper and pencil, a portable calculator is the better aid. For those who say, 'But what if you don't have a calculator?' the appropriate answer is, 'So what if you don't have paper and pencil?' In either situation, you would estimate the answer or borrow the technology, and a calculator is now readily available in almost any group setting."[3] Sylwester continues, "We should concentrate more on developing our students' ability to quickly locate, estimate, organize, and interpret information, and we should teach them how to use the superior speed and accuracy of available information technologies whenever a complex problem requires an accurate solution. HyperCard Stacks, spread sheets, statistical programs, and spell checkers are only a few examples of the rapidly developing software programs that can assist our imprecise brains in solving problems and communicating ideas with detailed accuracy."[4]

CHANGING OUR POINT OF VIEW

Technology is changing the way we look at life in general. As I type these words into my computer, newer, faster, and more effective machines and programs are being made available. Therefore, it is not my intent to list specific software programs, the newest hardware, or a list of powerful Internet sites or World Wide Web addresses to support you in your teaching of mathematics. Most likely, they would change by the time you read this book. Instead, let's look at how technology has and can become a tool for us as professional educators.

So where do we begin? Let's take a look at what the NCTM standards say about technology. According to NCTM, "Because technology is changing mathematics and its uses we believe that:

- Appropriate calculators should be available to all students at all times

- A computer should be available in every classroom for demonstration purposes

- Every student should have access to a computer for individual and group work

- Students should learn to use the computer as a tool for processing information and performing calculations to investigate and solve problems."[5]

It is clear that the NCTM standards support the use of technology in the classroom, but this is only the beginning. What should it look like in the classroom?

First Things First: Taking Inventory of Ourselves as Users of Technology

An interesting reality is that we live in an "AC/BC" world. Individuals born before 1977 are "BC" (born Before Computers), while individuals born after 1977 are "AC" (born After Computers). This translates to mean that all teachers are "BC people" and all students in 1996 are "AC people." According to Mark Share, Director of Educational Technology, Scottsdale, Arizona, "There is a distinction between most AC/BC people in terms of how they may perceive the world in terms of technology. BC people may always feel as though they're trying to catch up on the latest technology and to overcome some fears associated with it. AC people have no fear and are more able to apply what they've learned from one program to another."[6] As time goes on, and the "AC kids" of this country become teachers, this distinction will begin to diminish in our schools. Meanwhile, for those of us BC people who have not yet made the leap, the discomfort level will continue to grow.

Before we can expect our students to become proficient users of math and related technologies, we must become learners and be on our own personal journey toward proficiency. To take inventory of where we are, to assess our attitudes and proficiencies, consider the research by Apple Classrooms of Tomorrow (ACOT). ACOT found that teachers progress through five stages of development that range from just beginning to the advanced user. Use this list as a self-assessment tool to determine how you are doing regarding technology use and application at the present time and to create an action plan in determining "next steps."

- **Entry.** You are at entry level if you are struggling to learn about your new computer. Your computer is probably at home instead of at school where your students can't use it because you are afraid that anyone else who uses it will mess it up! You have a hard time giving yourself permission to "play" for fear of doing permanent damage.

"Teaching is the greatest act of optimism."

Colleen Wilcox

- **Adoption.** You are at the adoption level if you have brought your computer to school but you still are having a hard time letting students touch it. You use it for generating classroom materials and written correspondence. You might even be experimenting with basic programs (simple word processing) since you are beginning to realize that you really can't do anything to your computer that someone else can't fix.

- **Adaptation.** You are at the adaptation level if you have finally allowed students to have access to your computer. You are becoming more and more confident in your own use and are even allowing yourself to experiment with new software. Your classroom teaching might change a little due to a few ideas that you have had about using computers to help students accomplish their work.

- **Appropriation.** You are at the appropriation stage if you are using technology on a daily basis. You have discovered that the computer is truly a tool that can not only save you time but make your teaching more effective. Now when you come across a problem, you spend some time trying to figure it out on your own, and might even purchase some software for yourself or your students. You are confident that you can solve most of your own problems by "playing" with the program for a while.

- **Invention.** You are at the highest level of technology use, invention, if you are dependent upon technology in your teaching. You might not find software that will accomplish the things you want but you are able to use programs such as HyperCard, Persuasion, Multi-Media Presentations, etc., to produce materials that assist your teaching. Your students are using some of the same programs too![7]

It is important to remember that people may rate themselves at different levels based on the kind of technology being focused on. For example, if one is looking at the use of calculators or simple word processing applications for a personal computer, one may rate himself or herself at the invention level, but when it comes to the application of other technology such as use of the Internet or creating multi-media presentations, one may find himself or herself at the adoption level.

Keeping a Balanced Approach

Keeping a balanced approach in terms of how to use technology in your classroom is crucial. Remember, technology is a means to an end, not an end in itself. Also, and perhaps most importantly, technology can never be a replacement for an understanding of math or a sense of number-ness. Brain research makes it amply clear that technology cannot replace the nervous system as the conduit of experience upon which mathematical concepts and understandings are based. The graphic below illustrates a view of learning based upon brain research versus a mistaken view of the role of technology.

Technology use from the perspective of current brain research:

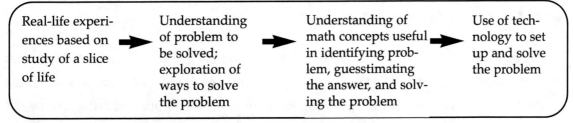

Typical view of use of technology with typical results:

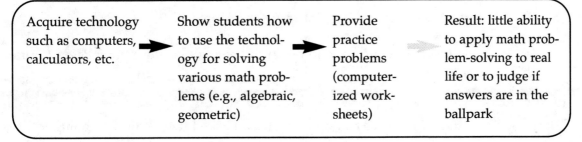

We must look at how and why we teach basic skills to our students. We must teach enough skills so that students will know if their results from the technology are reasonable. Students must have enough knowledge to check answers. If a student enters 55 x 20 into the calculator and comes up with an answer of 250, does the student know enough to recognize that an error has been made or just assumes it must be correct because that's what the calculator shows?

Software selection is another important issue. If you assign a software program for your students to work on just because they like it, rather than because it carries out your instructional goal, you are then allowing the software to mandate what you're trying to accomplish instead of you yourself dictating what you want your students to learn and how they can best learn it. When this happens, the teacher is essentially surrendering the control of what happens in his or her classroom to the machine. It's not about the piece of software, but what your instructional goal is and how a specific piece of software will help your students achieve this goal.

You may be reading this chapter and thinking to yourself, "I agree, technology in the classroom is a must but I only have access to one computer (or maybe not even that) at my school." Unfortunately, it is a reality that some districts have more technology than others. However, remember back about fifteen years ago. At that time, hand-held calculators were so expensive that only some teachers and richer districts could afford them. Now, their prices have come down and are affordable for most people. The same was true for VCR's. As this trend continues, computers, math-rich software, and multi-media will become less expensive and more attainable for all of us.

NOT ALL TECHNOLOGIES ARE NEW

Don't think of technology as being limited to the latest computer equipment, laser disk or satellite-connected something-or-other. There is one piece of technology that most students have access to but may not know how to use appropriately, the telephone. Although a sightless source for gathering information, the math possibilities are virtually endless. Just think of how reliant we adults are upon this familiar form of technology. We should help students learn to use it and its accouterments well.

How many students in your class do not know how to use the Yellow Pages to find information? Let me share a scenario that happened in my own classroom of second and third graders. While planning for a learning celebration in our classroom, my students approached me and asked if we could order pizza. I asked them who was going to pay for this and how much would it cost? They assured me that they could each bring in one dollar and they would call the local pizza delivery service. How could they be sure one dollar would be enough or too much money? I told them that they could order pizza if they completed the following process:

1. Survey class members to find out first and second choices for kind of pizza to be ordered. Tally and chart group results.

2. Formulate questions that will need to be asked of pizza delivery service. Some of the questions my students came up with included, "How many slices in a small, medium, large, and extra large pizza? What is the diameter of each size? (There may be more slices from one pizzeria than from another, but they may be smaller!) What are the prices of each size with the desired topping? Do any of the pizza places offer discounts with coupons? If so, where does one find a coupon? Is there a limit to the number of coupons allowed per order? How much money can be saved? What will a piece of pizza cost per slice? Does the cost go up or down depending on the size of pizza ordered?

3. Use the Yellow Pages to look up the numbers of three pizza delivery services. (At this point the class was divided into three different groups based on which pizza delivery service was an individual's favorite. Each group, armed with a set of phone books, accessed a different phone in our school and began their research.)

4. Introduce yourself to the person on the other end of the telephone and explain your pizza research questions and what you are trying to do.

5. After gathering data, each group must construct a visual way using mathematics to show their findings to their classmates in the remaining two groups. Evidence of at least four original research questions must be reflected in the presentation.

6. Based on each group's findings, the class must then vote on which pizza delivery service they wanted and be able to defend their reasons to me.

7. Figure out how much money each person must contribute to our pizza party.

This pizza project took nearly a week but there were so many benefits ranging from real-life math application to working together to solve a problem! How many times as teachers do we simply pick up the phone and do the groundwork for our students? By teaching students to use the telephone to gather and access information, we are giving them tools to better use the kind of technology with which they are already very familiar!

THE BOTTOM LINE

Learning to use technology to solve problems in the "real" world, rather than for rote drill, requires skills necessary for all of us to acquire in order to survive in our society.

"Thus, the challenge in technological problem solving isn't merely to teach students how to use computers—how to touch-type and navigate through files—but also to understand the nature of computerized information, and the social, political, and ethical issues that computers create."[8]

It's not about technology either; it's about life!

For Further Study

Technopoly : The Surrender of Culture to Technology by Neil Postman

Information Anxiety: What To Do When Information Doesn't Tell You What You Need to Know by Richard Wurman

Chapter 7
Girls and Math:

Gender Equity

A look at math education is not complete without a look at gender bias. When we look at the ratio of boys to girls in higher level math classes in high school and in college, it is easy to see that the results are not equal. Not only are there more boys but they tend to receive higher grades as well. When we look at math-oriented careers, they are also dominated by males. Why is this so? Why does there seem to be a "glass ceiling" for girls and math? Where does gender bias come from? How does math instruction in the elementary grades contribute to it? What is gender equity?

It has been twenty-four years since the passage of Title IX, prohibiting discrimination on the basis of sex in any educational programs receiving federal funds. And yet, after a quarter of a century of consciousness raising and millions of dollars thrown at the issue, "girls and boys are still not on equal footing in our nation's classrooms."[1] Furthermore, "girls and boys are mixed together in our schools but they are not receiving the same quality or quantity of education—nor are they genuinely learning from and about each other."[2] Many experts tell us that there are numerous reasons for this: sexist lessons, womanless history or only a few token women in history; the kinds of toys that are chosen for us as children; girls' learning problems not being identified as often as boys', boys receiving more of their teacher's attention; not as many female role models, stereotypes of who should become doctors and engineers; and societal and peer

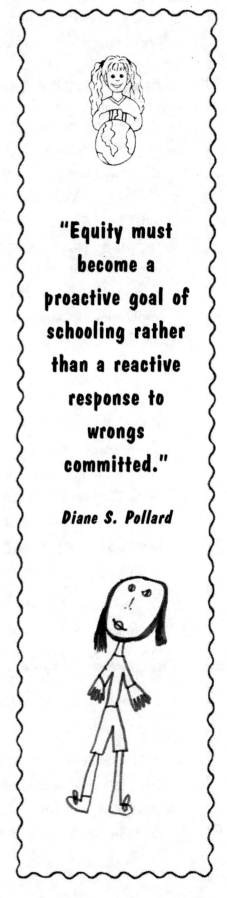

"Equity must become a proactive goal of schooling rather than a reactive response to wrongs committed."

Diane S. Pollard

expectations. The problem is so endemic that these causes—each powerful and substantial—are but the tip of the iceberg.

GENDER EQUITY AND BRAIN RESEARCH

The tendency for expectations to turn into final results has been well known for some time. Now, brain research suggests yet another reason for taking gender equity seriously. If a learner doesn't see the information or skill to be learned as meaningful for his or her life (as perceived by the learner, not the teacher), the brain doesn't fully activate. Girls must be able to apply math to roles that they currently see themselves in and may currently be participating in: cooking, interior design, sewing, economics of child rearing, automotive costs, housing costs, clothing, household budgets, and shopping. Once they see how math can empower them in current roles, it is easier for them to see math applications in areas that they may not originally see as their own. (For a down-to-earth discussion of the power of emotions and expectations of others to shut down learning, see *ITI: The Model* by Susan Kovalik, pages 17-34.)

In her book, *Reviving Ophelia: Saving the Selves of Adolescent Girls*, Dr. Mary Piper reports that "When boys have trouble with a math problem, they are more likely to think the problem is hard but stay with it. When girls have trouble, they think they are stupid and tend to give up. This difference in attribution speaks to girls' precipitous decline in math. Girls need to be encouraged to persevere in the face of difficulty, to calm down and believe in themselves. They need permission to take their time and to make many mistakes before solving the problem. They need to learn relaxation skills to deal with the math anxiety so many experience."[3]

The topic of gender bias alone could fill numerous volumes of books. It is not my intent to do so here. But, this book would not be complete if I did not mention it or at least offer several resources in an attempt to bridge this gap. To begin, we must help girls see how math could empower them in what they currently do. Next, we must give them windows upon the world, opportunities to see other females in roles requiring extensive use of math.

The bottom line is this: Gender equity is not about doing more for girls and less for boys. It is about eliminating the barriers and stereotypes that limit the opportunities and choices of both sexes. The following resources and materials are a beginning step in exploring issues of gender in mathematics in elementary schools.

RESOURCES FOR GIRLS AND MATH

Bridgewater State College
Department of Mathematics and Computer Science
Bridgewater, MA 02325
508/697-1341
E-mail: price@bridgew.edu

Will e-mail a bibliography on girls and math and science upon request. Also holds a summer program for girls in math and physics.

The National Coalition of Girls' Schools
228 Main Street
Concord, MA 01742
508/287-4485
E-mail: NCGS@delphi.com

Organizes conferences on girls and math and publishes symposia proceedings and other material available free of charge.

EQUALS
240 Lawrence Hall
University of California
Berkeley, CA 94720
510/642-1823

Provides teacher training and curricular materials to promote females in math courses and careers. Publishes a teacher education program, classroom activities, and curriculum for grades 1-8.

The Equity Institute
P.O. Box 30245
Bethesda, MD 20824
301/654-2904

Provides videos and a series of books aimed at grades 1-4, featuring girls who overcome gender, race, and ethnic barriers to forge careers in math and science.

Women in Mathematics Education
Mt. Holyoke College
302 Shattuck Hall
South Hadley, MA 01075
413/538-2608; FAX: 413/538-2002
E-mail: cmorrow@mhe.bitnet

Publishes a newsletter, a bibliography, and a directory for an annual membership fee. Also sponsors a summer math program for girls.

For Further Study

How to Encourage Girls in Math and Science (Grades K-8)
by J. Skolnick, C. Langbort, and L. Day

Failing at Fairness by Myra and David Sadker

Chapter 8
Integrating Math:

The Final Frontier

For many educators, math seems to be the "final fron-tier," the last subject to be included into their integration of curriculum. Our math phobia leads us to believe that although other mortals might be able to integrate math, we can't, couldn't, wouldn't. . . unthinkable! If you find your-self in this category (as I found myself), fear no longer!

Much to my surprise, integrating math is simple if we follow one golden rule: base your math instruction and practice on real life situations, events, and places that students can experience firsthand during your instruction. Plan experiences that are innately engaging to your students and that elicit maximum sensory processing by the brain. In other words, don't base instruction on content or examples from life that your students might have expe-rienced in the past or on content that is presented second-hand, e.g., books, videos, etc.

The brain processes best in "here and now" situations from real life, not fabricated, secondhand tales. If you follow this golden rule, you will not only meet the demands of the human brain but you will discover that integration of subject area content occurs naturally. No strain, no pushing and pulling of this part of this subject with that part of that subject. And math, like science, is everywhere the eye looks. Whether you are teaching about a place, animals, plants, or an event, you will always be able to incorporate times, dates, distances, measurement, or growth, etc. Statistics, from real life, are all you need to integrate math into your curriculum effectively—in any and all subject areas.

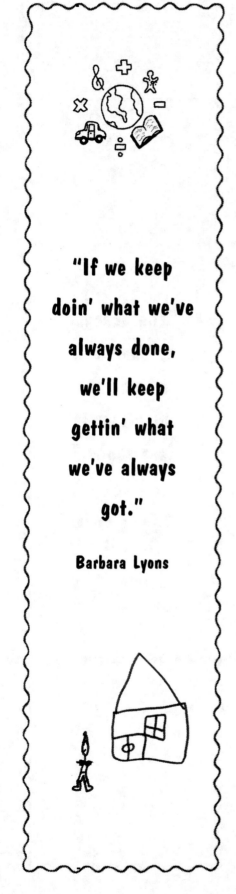

"If we keep doin' what we've always done, we'll keep gettin' what we've always got."

Barbara Lyons

"The absence
of change is
worse than
inaction, it
is atrophy."

Carolyn Warner

To help you "find the math" for every component of study, ask yourself common sense questions such as the following:

- How long did it take?

- How much did it cost?

- How much did it weigh?

- Which is greater or less than?

- What are the categories each item belongs to?

- How long will it take you to get there?

- How much more did it weigh than your estimate (or another object)?

- How big is it? How does it compare in size/weight/area to a _____?

- What are the dimensions of the object?

- How much area is involved?

- How many people will be involved?

- When will the event happen again?

- How far is it?

- How much will it cost?

- How could I have cut my costs?

- How much time elapsed between ____ and ____?

- Etc. (Let the curiosity of the child within you lead the questioning; the possibilities are endless.)

The list above is not complete, nor should it ever be. You may already be thinking of numerous questions to add to the list. Ask your students to help you ask the right questions.

Once math is fully integrated, it takes two forms: "theme math" which uses the content of the theme to make mathematics come alive and be more understandable conceptually and "skillshops" through which the teacher zeroes in on specific basic skills that students need to work on.

THEME MATH

The purpose of theme math is to build conceptual understanding of mathematical concepts and operations, not to drill or press for rote memory. It is a time to demonstrate for students the power of mathematics to extract greater meaning and understanding from the information at hand than would be possible without the application of math as a tool, as a means to greater understanding and thus more powerful decision making.

For examples of theme math, see the following chapters:

- Chapter 9: Practical Applications: Theme Math

- Chapter 10: Practical Applications: Math Challenges in the Real World—Places and Events

- Chapter 11: Practical Applications: Micro Communities

SKILLSHOP

Over the years, many teachers have asked me, "But when do I just teach the skill?" Here is what I recommend.

Daily Skillshops

Although math will be happening throughout the day, you probably have a block of time that you devote to math instruction. I had a forty-five minute time block set aside for this at the end of each day. I devoted two or three days of the week during this time to the teaching or reteaching of a particular skill during "Skillshop." During the remaining two or three days of the week, I focused on how to use this skill in relation to our theme in terms of application to real-world situations, e.g., if a group of students in my class, or perhaps my entire class, were ready to learn the skill of double-digit addition with regrouping, I might devote three days (or more if I needed to do so) during my math block on the actual teaching of that skill. I would use everything I knew about applying Howard Gardner's theory of the multiple intelligences to teach children the patterns needed to understand and apply the skill and then create a mental program for storage in long-term memory.

Once the children understood how to execute the skill, the remaining two or three days of the week during this math block would be used to focus on how we could use that skill during study of our theme. The key point about the integration of mathematics into your curriculum is this: *The integration of individual skills of mathematics occurs through their application—how you ask your students to use them as tools to better understand the content they are studying.*

"Concept in a Day" Skillshops

Brain research regarding the importance of ample practice in order to reach mastery and longterm memory is quite convincing. Thus another way to teach a concept and its computational skill at the same time is to provide an intensive, all-day experience. Martha Kaufeldt modeled how that can be done with long division. With her class of 30 fourth graders (plus twenty other fifth and sixth graders who had failed long division), Martha moved 50 students to mastery in one day. Fortunately, that day was captured on video. *I Can Divide and Conquer* provides a window into her day that has allowed teachers all across the country to replicate her success.

Mastery of long division in one day! Impossible you say. It seems so because with traditional instruction, "it is estimated that it takes two years and three months for students to learn long division. The division facts are introduced in the third grade, the algorithm is introduced in the fourth grade, again in the fifth and sixth grades."[2] By providing students an opportunity to have numerous and varied input about the patterns and real-life applications of long division and by giving them plenty of immediate feedback, students were able to master the concept of long division in one day! Posttests given the following day showed that some students improved as much as 150 percent. Posttests given three months later showed continued improvement and retention. For more information about how to implement this concept, I recommend the book and companion videotape, *I Can Divide and Conquer: A Concept in a Day!* by Martha Miller Kaufeldt. (These and other related materials are available through Books For Educators.)

Division in a day is only the beginning. Schools across the country have conducted Punctuation Day, Multiplication Week, and Quotation Mark Day. The content possibilities of the daylong skillshop are unlimited.

For Further Study

ITI: The Model
by Susan Kovalik with Karen Olsen

I Can Divide and Conquer: A Concept in a Day (book and video)
by Martha Miller Kaufeldt

Classroom of the 21st Century (book and video)
by Robert Ellingsen

Chapter 9
Practical Applications:

Theme Math

Theme math is a two-way street. Its purpose is first to build conceptual understanding of math—the four operations and each of the strands identified by NCTM—through real world studies and then to experience the additional knowledge that comes from studying content using mathematical tools to analyze and interpret information. Theme math is not a time to drill on memorization of facts and computations; it is a time to generate the desire to compute.

Theme math is also a time to experience what it means to think mathematically without the barrier of weak computation skills getting in the way. According to Robert Ellingsen, "Students who do not have their multiplication facts memorized are still capable of understanding the concept of multiplication. Memorization of facts should not be a prerequisite to opportunities for applying concepts. If anything, building the concepts should come first, giving the student the meaningful framework before the individual skill bits are put into place."[1]

EXAMPLES OF MATH CONTENT FOR THEMES

Math is the ultimate hitchhiker; it can travel anyone's road, work and play with any theme. The following examples illustrate numerous possibilities for math integration within the theme. They are not intended to redirect a theme you may be developing; their purpose is to illustrate how omnipresent math opportunities are and how easily they can be captured. Also highlighted are ways to integrate math with community service projects, individual research projects, and newspaper and magazine resources.

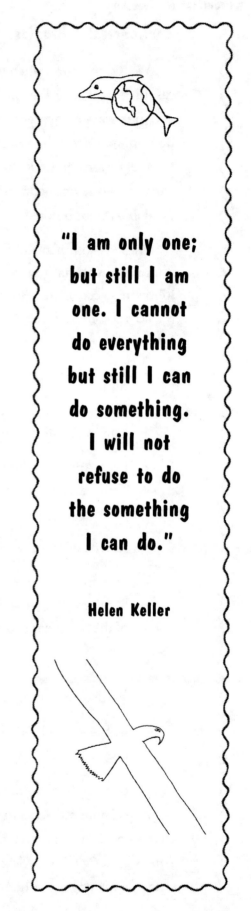

"I am only one; but still I am one. I cannot do everything but still I can do something. I will not refuse to do the something I can do."

Helen Keller

Environmental Studies

We live in a time when the population of our planet is ever increasing, yet the natural resources that we have, are not. The air we breathe is not as pure as the air of 150 years ago, our waters have become polluted, we are filling up more and more landfills each day, and our protective ozone layer is weakening, to name but a few troublesome facts. Virtually every grade level contains science concepts relevant to this topic. (For a user-friendly K-6 science curriculum, see *Continuum of Science Concepts, K-6* by Karen Olsen; available through Books for Educators.)

There is so much to be done and so many powerful opportunities to give children important real math application opportunities that have relevance and meaning. The following facts, filled with mathematical implications, are from the book, *50 Simple Things Kids Can Do To Save The Earth.* They are examples of the "math" to be found everywhere for every subject area.

- As a nation, we use over 65 billion aluminum soda cans every year!

- The energy you save from recycling just one aluminum can could keep your TV running for three hours!

- Each American throws away about 60 pounds of plastic packaging every year! Think about how much you weigh. Now think about how much 60 pounds of plastic is.

- Americans use 2.5 million plastic bottles every hour. Most of them get thrown away.

- Styrofoam is permanent garbage. It can't ever become part of the earth again. Five hundred years from now a boy might be digging in his backyard and find a piece of the Styrofoam cup from which you drank lemonade at yesterday's picnic!

- Every year each of us tosses out about 1,200 pounds of organic garbage.

- We use millions of feet of paper towels every year. That's a lot of trees!

- In one year a leaky toilet can waste over 22,000 gallons of water. That's enough to take three baths every day![2]

Unfortunately, I could go on and on. Helping to take care of our planet is crucial and provides unlimited ways to make sense of math. Kids can show their findings by making charts and graphs of what they've discovered. I highly recommend this book, *50 Simple Things Kids Can Do To Save The Earth,* for further investigation. For examples of how students can engage in home-centered math explorations, see Chapter 13.

Economics Studies

Learning about the stock market is one way to gain a more in-depth understanding of the economy at large. Students in grades 5-12 can participate in the stock market by playing "The Stock Market Game" developed in 1977 by the Securities Industry Association (SIA). "The Stock Market Game" is a unique educational tool that helps students build skills in a wide range of disciplines. Beyond business and math, this motivational tool is used to teach social studies, language arts, life skills, science, and economics. Watch your students' skills grow as they have fun meeting the challenge of learning more about the stock market and the world of finance through this intriguing game.

To play the game, student teams, up to five members, are each given a hypothetical $100,000 to invest in common stocks listed on the New York and American Stock Exchanges and the NASDAQ National Market System. Each week during this 10 week game, teams receive a portfolio which shows the transactions placed, brokerage commissions, interest on margin loans paid, and their rank based on portfolio equity.

Through the Stock Market Game, students develop:

- an ability to integrate mathematics, social studies, and reading and to apply these subjects to daily decisions

- an understanding of how the stock market works

- an understanding of how basic economic and business concepts relate to market conditions

- an understanding of how political and economic events affect stock choices and price

- an ability to utilize the newspaper to gather information and make decisions

There are currently 500,000 students participating in 48 states on an annual basis. Competition is divided between grades 5-8 and 9-12. Three to five students make up a team. The registration fee for teams to participate is $16.00 per team. For more information call Business Economics Education Foundation of Minnesota (BEEF), 612/337-5252 Monday-Friday.

To help children understand consumer economics by being a real consumer in their immediate world, consider creating an ongoing micro-community at your school. Such micro-community provide real and meaningful consumer decision-making opportunities for students in a low-risk, small consequences environment and on a daily basis. For further information, please refer to Chapter 11.

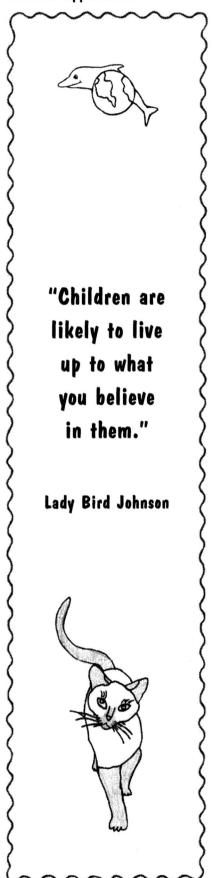

"Children are likely to live up to what you believe in them."

Lady Bird Johnson

Fine Arts

Relating fractions to reading and writing music offers natural opportunities to show students the interrelatedness of music and math. At the same time that you teach fractional parts, you or a music teacher can introduce how to read music. The signature and structure of the notes are good examples of the interrelatedness of music and math, e.g., 3/4 or 4/4 time, whole and half notes, quarter, eighth, sixteenth notes, and thirty-secondth notes. To assess if your students understand this correlation, you may ask them to compose a song using a specific number of quarter notes, half notes, etc. or count the number of such notes in five or six bars of a popular song.

Creating weavings or paintings illustrates the beauty of angles and shapes as they are mixed with color and/or texture. As part of a geometry study, students may be asked to discover pieces of art work that have various geometric characteristics. For example, "Find a piece of art composed of at least three right angles, two parallel lines, and one triangle."

Other math opportunities include gauging kiln temperatures and measuring plaster, dyes, paints, and water, etc. Figuring the percentages of money and/or materials to be used per project, and maintaining an art budget for the class are additional ways to use mathematical concepts.

As part of the preparation of the production of a theme-related class play, students can design and construct scale drawings of the set (also ratios), and then actually produce the sets as well.

Human Body Study

Study of the human body is a gold mine for math integration opportunities. In one of my favorite books, *Blood and Guts,* Linda Allison tells us that our bodies are many things:

- We are miles of blood vessels, billions of cells, hundreds of muscles, thousands of hairs, and quarts of blood.

- Sixty percent of our bodies are made up of water.

- A square patch of skin, 3/4 inch x 3/4 inch, is only about one-twentieth of an inch thick yet contains: 9 feet of blood vessels, 600 pain sensors, 30 hairs, 300 sweat glands, 4 oil glands, 13 yards of nerves, 9,000 nerve endings, 6 cold sensors, 35 heat sensors, and 75 pressure sensors.

- Collectively your hair grows altogether 1,000 inches per day. The average head has 100,000 hairs.

- An eyelash lives about 150 days.

- You have three different kinds of muscles in your body, altogether more than 600 muscles.

- Humans have a high-performance heart that averages about 2.5 billion beats per lifetime.

- The heart circulates the body's blood more than 1,000 times per day.

- Each kidney contains about one-million tiny tubes which add up to more than 40 miles in length.

- Each day 180 quarts of blood are pumped through the kidneys. That's 25% of the blood pumped through your heart or as much blood as flows through 100 pounds of muscle.[3]

The list above represents only a few of the amazing facts about our bodies. There is so much information about the different parts of your body, in which math integration possibilities are screaming out at you, that entire books could be written about them! In fact, numerous books have already been written!

Practical Applications

Whether you are learning about the human body in a general way or specifically investigating one system, questions such as the following will help you uncover even more math:

- How many bones including vertebrate do we have? Categorize them by geometric shape.

- How much blood do we have? Does the amount increase as we grow?

- What is the average life span for men? For women? Is it the same in other parts of the world?

- What are the average heights and weights for men? For women? Is it the same in other parts of the world?

- What is the average percentage of body fat for men? For women?

- What range of blood pressure is considered average or normal? Does it ever change? How? Why? At what levels is it considered dangerous?

- What is the correlation of pulse and physical activity?

- How do we measure a person's eyesight or hearing? Compare both to that of a local species of owl.

According to *The Science Continuum of Concepts*, K-6, by Karen Olsen, an in-depth study of the human body would be appropriate in the sixth grade. This study will lead to a more complex understanding of how your body works and how to best take care of it.

Animal Studies

For any kind of in-depth study about a particular animal, students can design and build a habitat or model of a habitat for that animal. This provides meaningful practice in the concepts of measurement and ratio, as well as basic computation.

Understanding habitats also necessitates an understanding of the effects of climate and weather. Specific animals will not survive if their habitat becomes too warm or too cold, too wet or too dry, or provides too much sun or shade and so forth. Special attention must be given to these concerns. Have students analyze the habitat of an animal from another country to determine where and if that animal could survive in their local area (for older students, elsewhere in the United States).

Estimating and calculating miles flown or swum during migration or time spent hibernating, are additional springboards for math integration. Compare this information to how many miles and how much time your students spend traveling back and forth to school or on a family vacation.

Exploring the entire species of animals being studied is another opportunity for math integration. Is the animal being studied endangered? How many are left? What is the reproduction cycle of the animal? How long is the gestation period? How much does the animal eat daily, weekly, etc.? Are some animal populations greater in some areas than in others? Why? Is this animal in danger of being placed on the endangered list in the future? Why? All of these questions require an understanding of math concepts to investigate.

Hatching chicks or ducks in an incubator as part of a study of birds can provide a springboard for many mathematical inquiries. Students can estimate the length of time they think it will take for the eggs to hatch. This can be compared and contrasted to the actual incubation time. By recording daily readings of the temperature and humidity levels inside the incubator, you will have numerical data to calculate the range, mode, median, and mean of your estimations and readings during the incubation time.

Many teachers incorporate the study of a child's pet into his or her curriculum. This study usually focuses on the animal itself, its habitat, behaviors, and favorite things about the child's pet. Here's a twist you may not have incorporated before. How much does it cost to take care of this pet? How much does it cost daily, weekly, or annually to feed this pet? How often does the pet go to a groomer or veterinarian? What are the costs incurred? What are average annual bills? Do you have pet insurance for your pet? Is pet insurance affordable? What services will the insurance cover? Do all veterinarians in your area charge the same fees? Why or why not? Students may want to interview local veterinarians and keep a written record of how much they are feeding their own pets to learn the answers to these questions.

For supplemental ideas for studies of zoo animals, please refer to, Chapter 10, Math Opportunities: Events and Places.

Insect Studies

If you're looking for large numbers to play with, insects are for you! Did you know that there are about five million different kinds of insects in the world? Consider the following facts from the *Eyewitness Juniors Book*: *Amazing Insects and Amazing Butterflies and Moths:*

"A candle loses nothing of its light by lighting another candle."

James Keller

- An insect's body has three sections: head, thorax, and abdomen.

- Most insects live probably less than a year. Some adult mayflies live only for a few hours.

- A queen termite may lay eggs for up to 15 years and then die from exhaustion!

- Dragonflies can spot the movement of another insect up to 33 feet away; they have four wings and can fly up to 25 miles per hour.

- Flies have only two wings and can fly about 5 miles per hour.

- Ants may walk 1,000 feet from their nest to gather food, a very long way for their size, the equivalent for humans of walking 40 miles to the grocery store! Then, ants have to carry their food back with them to their nest.

- It takes a caterpillar about one minute to eat a leaf that is two inches long.

- There are about 20,000 different kinds of butterflies and about 150,000 kinds of moths in the world.

- The biggest moths and butterflies are the size of birds. With its wings open, a giant Atlas Moth may measure one foot across!

- The monarch butterfly can fly 80 miles per day as it travels its long migration route.[4]

Use these fascinating facts to enrich your students' math application opportunities while engaged in the study of insects. By estimating, comparing, and calculating, your students can have unlimited problem-solving situations, all in the process of showing you what they know about insects. Young children may be involved in counting, classifying, and sorting investigations while older students may be creating models of different insects to scale, counting how many miles a given insect can travel in a given amount of time, or computing how many species of an insect live in your area. You can take any of these facts to use to compare to the students themselves. For example, a grasshopper can leap as far as 30 inches. A tiny flea can jump 12 inches; the equivalent jump for a human would be jumping three or four city blocks!

Geographical Studies

When learning about a geographical location, the study of the economics of the city, state, or country is another easy way to integrate mathematical concepts and provide numerous application opportunities. Studying demographics and business information via statistics allows the data collector, researcher, and reader to gain a clearer understanding of the targeted place. Comparing this information with other geographical locations invites students to speculate why the data may be similar or different.

On the following pages, I have included charts and graphs from *Market Facts*, a publication by The Business Journal, in Phoenix, Arizona, which provide information about the Phoenix business market.

As you can see, the possibilities for using this information are limitless, no matter what your grade level. Now, let's look at the actual geography of the location being studied. Natural opportunities to explore include: creating maps to scale, creating a travel itinerary of the region in miles and travel time, and preparing a budget for the trip while figuring out monetary amounts in the given country's currency and what it would be worth in U.S. dollars.

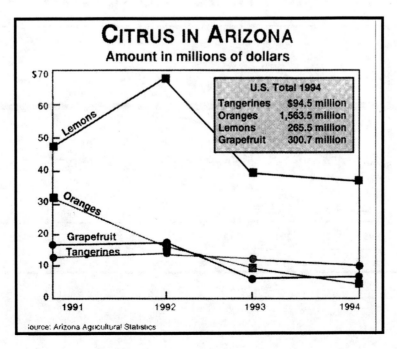

AGE OF MARICOPA COUNTY RESIDENTS

Age	1995	2000	2025	2045
0-9	381,248	414,817	605,593	803,202
10-19	323,449	376,434	557,203	749,378
20-29	351,206	362,296	563,434	772,461
30-49	751,009	835,268	1,085,077	1,431,680
50-64	300,204	392,112	771,583	989,343
65-79	240,339	261,938	644,246	768,887
80+	77,092	99,094	189,908	419,087
Total	2,424,547	2,741,959	4,417,044	5,934,038

1995 percentages

- 0-9 15.7%
- 10-19 13.3%
- 20-29 14.5%
- 30-49 31%
- 65-79 9.9%
- 80+ 3.2%
- 50-64 12.4%

Source: Arizona Department of Economic Security, Population Statistics Unit

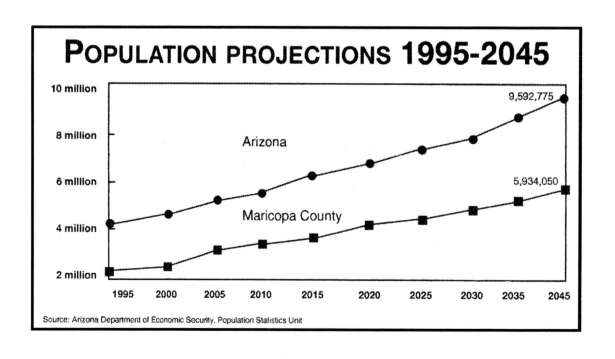

POPULATION PROJECTIONS 1995-2045

Arizona 9,592,775

Maricopa County 5,934,050

10 million
8 million
6 million
4 million
2 million

1995 2000 2005 2010 2015 2020 2025 2030 2035 2045

Source: Arizona Department of Economic Security, Population Statistics Unit

VALLEY LIFESTYLES

	Households participating	% of all households in market
Subscribe to cable TV	638,547	56.8%
Watching sports on TV	471,041	41.9
Own a dog	446,309	39.7
Avid book reading	445,184	39.6
Use a personal computer	439,563	39.1
Camping/hiking	369,863	32.9
Own a cat	286,672	25.5
Golf	257,442	22.9
Bicycling frequently	232,710	20.7
Travel for business	215,847	19.2
Casino gambling	212,474	18.9
Attend cultural/arts events	156,264	13.9
Recreational vehicles	130,408	11.6
Running/jogging	121,414	10.8
Boating/sailing	105,675	9.4

Source: *The Lifestyle Market Analyst 1995*, produced by National Demographics and Lifestyles, Denver, and SRDS, Des Plaines, Ill.

Americans come from many backgrounds. Exploring the ancestry of your class is another way to look at statistics. Compiling data by surveying the cultural heritage of your students and then charting and graphing the results will give your students an opportunity to know each other better and provide opportunities to interpret numerical data. On the following two pages, I have included some samples of how this was done by Mary DeVincenzi's fifth grade class in Rohnert Park, California.

Students can develop their own graphs of major waves of immigration to the U.S. from the 1800s (or any other given date) to the present. This information can be used to predict future immigration trends.

Exploring the architecture associated with a geographical location allows for identification and application opportunities of geometry. What are the predominant shapes and/or angles used to design and construct structures of a particular time and/or place? Do you see a similar kind of architecture used in the community where you live? What is the foundation for your answer?

Practical Applications

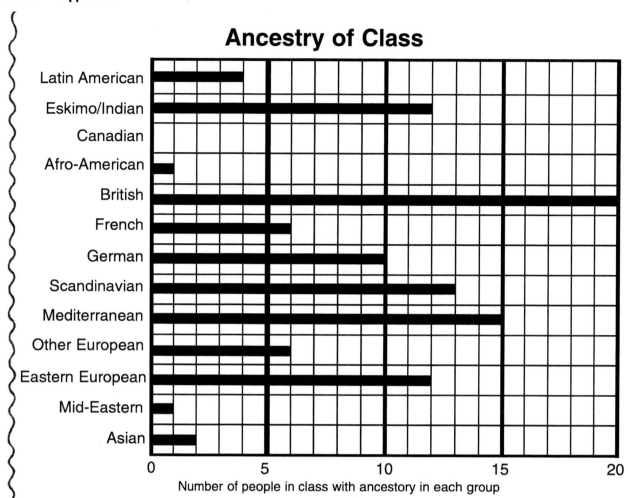

Ancestry of Class

Number of people in class with ancestry in each group

Our Heritage

Mexican	|||	Scotch-Irish	||	Dutch	||||
Guatemalan			Black Irish			Portuguese	||
Blackfeet			Welsh			Armenian		
Choctaw			French	卌		Czech		
Cherokee	卌			German	卌 卌	Lithuanian		
Osage			Danish	||	Polish	||||
Sioux			Finish	||	Russian	||||
Upper Skail			Norwegian	||	Ukrainian		
Black American			Swedish	卌 ||	Jordanian		
English	卌 卌 卌		Italian	卌 卌 |||	Chinese		
Irish	卌 卌 卌 ||	Spanish	||	Korean		
Scottish	卌 |||				

Mary DeVincenzi's classroom Rohnert Park,CA

86

Plants and Flowers

Planting seeds and growing plants or flowers provide numerous ways to integrate math. Before you begin actually planting, students can predict how tall their plant will be, how long it will take the seed to germinate and bloom. Students may keep a special journal and calendar to record this information.

Watering a plant regularly is very important. Keeping a watering schedule will help students learn how to successfully care for a living plant. If plants have been planted outside, keeping track of the weather conditions will allow students to understand why their plants have or have not grown.

Keep a permanent growth chart "attached" to the plant. Have students create their own measuring tape on a piece of paper or tag board. Post this on the wall next to the growing plant and provide a popsicle stick or other type of support for the plant. As the plant grows, it will climb up the measuring tape for easy readability. This way the student will not have to handle the plant to record its growth, thus keeping the plant healthier. Doing leaf drawings periodically will show students the symmetry and patterns in the leaves and how they develop.

RESOURCES

Resources for math opportunities in the real world are everywhere. Start with the kinds of resources you use in your own life to get through your day. Magazines, newspapers, the Yellow Pages, billboards, radio . . . .

Magazine Resources

Sometimes the integration of math is inherent in the materials you are using as your resources. For example, Jean Spanko, a teacher in Scottsdale, Arizona, taught her middle school students about the "Power of Persuasion," a monthly component of a yearlong theme entitled "Plugging Into Power." One of the topics studied was propaganda. After an introduction to propaganda and an exploration of its techniques, the students were asked to choose a magazine and then figure out the percentage of the magazine devoted to advertising. The students were given this hint as a reminder: "Find the page total of the entire magazine, then add all the pages and fractions of pages that contain advertising. Divide the advertising total by the page total to get your percentage."

Practical Applications

Some magazines for children provide readily available math opportunities and resources. I recommend the following publications:

- *Zillions: Consumer Reports for Kids* tells kids how to earn money, manage an allowance, and compare products and prices. This publication for 8-14 year olds evaluates products and advertising aimed at them. Comments from kid testers make for fun reading. Subscription information: $16.00 a year (12 issues). Zillions, Subscription Department, P.O. Box 51777, Boulder, CO 80323-1777.

- *Sports Illustrated for Kids* provides funny sports photos, sports cards, and sports tips with accompanying stories about sports legends. The magazine keeps kids updated on scores, individual and team statistics, and salaries. Subscription information: $23.95 a year (12 issues). Phone number, 800/732-5005.

- *Cricket.* This magazine, offering literature and art from around the world, is filled with stories and historical data which is an easy way to integrate mathematical concepts. Subscription information: $32.97 a year (12 issues). Phone number, 800/827-0227.

- *National Geographic World* has geography, nature, outdoor adventure, science, and kids' accomplishments and is a favorite of 8-14 year olds. A great resource for finding data about our natural world. Subscription information: $14.95 a year (12 issues). Phone number, 800/NGS-LINE (800/647-5463).

- *Ranger Rick* is the most famous and popular nature-discovery magazine for children ages 6-12. It motivates young readers as it helps them understand the natural world. Individual subscriptions, $15. Ranger Rick's Nature Magazine, National Wildlife Federation, 8925 Leesburg Pike, Vienna, VA 22184-0001; fax number, 703/790-4400.

- *Math Scholastic* focuses on junior high level math. By Scholastic Inc., 555 Broadway, New York, NY 10012-3999. Subscription information, $6 a year (9 issues). Phone number, 212/343-6620.

- *U.S. Kids* provides current events, stories, games, and activities for children 5-12 with emphasis on health, nutrition, and safety. Individual subscriptions, $22, $3 per individual copy; 8 issues per year. Children's Better Health Institute, 1100 Waterway Blvd., Indianapolis, IN 46202-2156; fax number, 317/637-0126.

- *Cobblestone: The History Magazine for Young People* is an American history magazine for young people, ages 8-14, that helps them make sense of what is happening today. Individual subscription, $23. Cobblestone Publishing, Inc., 7 School St., Peterborough, NH 03458-1454. Phone number, 603/924-7209; fax number, 603/924-7380.

- *Zoobooks*. Each issue a full color overview of a particular animal or group of animals, e.g. apes, snakes, endangered animals, etc. Individual subscriptions, $19, $2 per copy. Wildlife Education, Inc., 9820 Willow Creek Road, Ste 300, San Diego, CA 92131-1112. Phone number, 619/745-0685.

Ask your school or local librarian for additional magazine resources to complement your curriculum.

The Local Newspaper As Resource

Your local newspaper offers a plethora of mathematical opportunities to be used. Reading and interpreting bar graphs, pie charts, and line graphs are only a few ways to access these opportunities. Figuring advertising rates and subscription costs and reading the classified ads show students how people get jobs, find housing, and do business. Many newspapers offer "Newspapers in Education" programs showing teachers how to teach all subjects and skills using their daily newspaper. "The use of money in advertising, the graphs of business profits, the data found in weather maps, the fractions in recipes, and the use of statistics in sports all show mathematics at work. A closer look through the newspaper reveals statements about the probability of events or current economic trends. Statistics appear in many articles and graphics illustrate shapes, symmetry, and angles. Rather than viewing fractions, decimals, monetary amounts, and measurement as isolated topics, students can see how these mathematics skills appear together in real problem situations."[5]

Math opportunities abound in each section of the newspaper:

Advertisements. Use advertisements to plan and budget for parties and meals, purchase gifts for a special occasion, solve problems, or calculate the actual cost of buying an advertisement. Remember to figure the variables of running an ad such as size of advertisement, use of more than one color of ink. Are you going to reprint a photo? How will this affect the price? What are the cost differentials among these decisions?

Practical Applications

Travel Section. Planning a vacation, whether it be a cruise, airplane flight, or car trip, are fun ways to incorporate mathematical concepts. Calculating hotel costs, food, distances traveled, arrival times and departures (don't forget about time zone changes), frequent flier miles earned, the most cost-effective way to redeem miles (upgrades? free tickets?), average cost of gasoline per gallon for a road trip, and miles per gallon are just the beginning.

Weather Section. Compare world, national, and local daily temperatures using temperature charts showing other days or locations; consult an almanac and compare; compare forecasts with actual data.

Food Section. Although we seldom think of the kitchen as a beehive of mathematics and chemistry, it is! Here are recipes, cooking times, and measurements galore. How much of each ingredient is needed to double, triple, or quadruple a recipe? How much will it cost to prepare a particular meal? Is it more economical to purchase store brands as opposed to national brands? Is the quality the same? What are the differences in nutritional values? What about organic versus commercial fruits and vegetables?

Sports Section. The Sports Section is a gold mine of statistical information, such as salaries per quarter, per game, annually; a player's statistics compared to the opposing team's player in the same position. How does the stadium or arena generate revenue to operate? What percentage of the revenue comes from concessions versus admissions? Does the team rely on private donations? How much does the team and/or the arena pay for taxes?

Classified Section. The Classified Section provides fascinating examples of data for number crunching. Below are examples of math explorations based on the "Newspapers in Education" program of the *Waco Tribune-Herald.*

- Find the part of the Classified Section that tells how much an ad costs per line. Choose a want ad. How much would that ad cost for four days? For eight days?

- Look through the Houses for Sale columns of the classified ads. Find five houses from different price ranges. Organize the ads in order of increasing price, starting with the lowest price. Look at the ad for the house with the highest price. Underline one thing that you think makes that house cost more than the others.

- Turn to the classified ads that offer land for sale. Cut out three ads that give both size and price. Figure price per square foot for each property. (One acre is 43,560 sq. ft.). For each ad, write a few sentences giving the reasons why the land has special value.

- Look in the Automotive Section of the classified ads. Decide on the car you would like to buy. Cut out five ads for that kind of car. Figure out the average price.

- Can you find ads for ten different makes of cars in the classified ads? Try to find cars from the same year. Cut out one of each and rank them by price, low to high.

- Turn to the Houses for Sale Section of the classified ads. Figure out the average cost per home for four different communities or parts of town. Base your average upon the first five listings in each area. Draw a bar graph that shows the average cost per home in each of the four areas.

- You have some toys to sell. Read some classified ads for Merchandise for Sale to see what kind of information is provided to readers. Write a four-line ad that will help sell your toys. If your paper prints an order form for Classifieds, fill that in.

For more information about a "Newspapers in Education" service in your area, please consult your local newspaper. For national newspapers, consider:

USA Today
Educational Development
1000 Wilson Blvd.
Arlington, VA 22091
800/USA-0001

The Washington Post
Educational Services Dept.
1150 Fifteenth Street, NW
Washington, D.C. 20071-7300
202/334-4544

COMMUNITY SERVICE PROJECTS

One of the most natural ways to integrate mathematics into your theme is through community service projects. Recycling, raising money for a specific charity, conserving water, cleaning up a neighborhood or the schoolyard, planting flowers to beautify an area, are just a few avenues for incorporating math, figuring such things as how much things cost, supply and demand, time = money, and how to raise funds. For more information about ideas for service projects for children, I recommend, *The Kids Guide to Social Action: How to Solve the*

"The greatest teacher is not the one who talks all the time but the one who listens."

Lauren, age 14

Social Problems YOU CHOOSE—and Turn Creative Thinking Into Positive Action, and *The Kids Guide to Service Projects: Over 500 Service Ideas for Young People Who Want To Make a Difference*, both written by Barbara A. Lewis. (Available from Books for Educators, 253/630-6908 or <www.books4educ.com/>)

Individual Research Projects

Individualized research projects, based on interest or theme, present another way to incorporate real life math into the student's life. A few years ago, I had a very bright third grade student who was a dedicated Phoenix Suns fan (I'll call him Bob). Bob was enthralled with the game of basketball and wanted to learn even more about it. That particular year, several students in my class worked on either trimester long or yearlong individualized research projects. Bob's project was to follow and record the statistics of Charles Barkley for the season. After each game, he would check the stats in the newspaper, cut them out, record them in his notebook, and finally figure averages and develop his own basketball card for Charles Barkley, all using the math skills he had learned in class. Almost all individualized research projects can be connected to the theme. In Bob's case, the major concept for our yearlong theme was that of interdependence. Bob had to be able to tell me at least three different ways that "Sir Charles" was interdependent with his team, the opposing team, the coaches, etc. If the connection to the theme is weak, it's a sure shot that the project can be connected through the Lifelong Guidelines and LIFESKILLS. (For a discussion of Lifelong Guidelines and LIFESKILLS, see *ITI: The Model* by Susan Kovalik or *The Way We Were...The Way We CAN Be: A Vision for the Middle School Through Integrated Thematic Instruction* by Ann Ross and Karen Olsen and Appendix B of this book).

Additional ways to incorporate mathematics into your theme can be explored in Chapters 10, 11, and 12. Please use these chapters as companions to each other. In summary, "Mathematical computation is still an essential life skill. Theme math does not replace that. But it does enhance computation by giving it meaning and purpose. Computation is still addressed. In fact, within this meaningful context of the theme, computation is learned much more readily."[6]

For Further Study

Eyewitness Junior Series

The Internet

Local Yellow Pages

Chapter 10
Practical Applications:

Math Challenges in the Real World—Places and Events

As we reflect on our own childhood and schooling, the memorable times are those associated with places we visited and events that we experienced. What makes them memorable is the high level of sensory input that comes with what we call "experience," doing something, going somewhere. In contrast, seat time activities were erased from (or never entered) our memory banks long ago.

Personally, the kinds of school experiences I can still remember from my own elementary and middle school years are the field trips I went on, the plays we performed, and projects I made. As I recall these experiences and field trips, and analyze the field trips I arranged as a classroom teacher, I realize that these trips were either science, social studies, or fine arts based. I don't recall ever hearing about a teacher taking his or her class on a "math field trip." Nor do I recall ever having "the math" of the location being pointed out. In fact, I don't think it was ever mentioned. What a crime! No wonder children's view of math is 'rithmetic, as textbook and dittos without end or relevance.

Math does not exist by itself as an abstract content to be studied only upon the printed page; it is an integral part of every aspect of our lives, every place we go, everything we do. All we need to do as teachers is point this out to students and structure opportunities to experience the truth of it for themselves. After a while, like the boy in *Math Curse*, students will begin to see everything as a math problem.

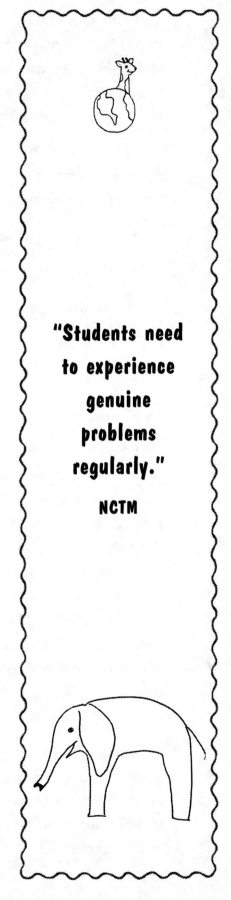

"Students need to experience genuine problems regularly."

NCTM

In this chapter, I have explored several common study trip locations that might also be available in your community. The information presented for each location or event clearly does not exhaust the potential of these "being there" opportunities to teach math; however, I hope you will find the framework below a useful tool when preparing to make math come alive for students.

For each location or event, I have provided some general background information and created a framework with categories that will help focus students' search for math in their everyday world. The categories are:

- significant information about the location

- physical characteristics of the location

- financial aspects

- inventory

- daily uses

- special events

Within each category are questions to expand students' thinking, to push them to probe beneath the surface of their experiences. Use these questions to support you in the development of extension possibilities once you return to the classroom. The "math possibilities" for grade levels K-3 and 4-6 ask students to apply math concepts in ways that help them analyze what they are learning at each location. Far from eliciting paper and pencil answers from students, these questions invite teacher introspection: How can students show, using this information, what they have learned and what can they do with it? Can they build a model of it to scale? Can they develop and propose a plan that would support the business/service in their efforts? Can students transfer their knowledge of how one place operates to their school or other place of business? Can students create charts or graphs to interpret their findings? Can students role-play a situation relating the experience to express what they know?

Although we typically associate certain field trips with a particular grade level, e.g., going to the firehouse at first grade, the zoo at second grade, etc., when we look at these locations from the perspective of understanding real-life uses of math, it becomes evident that these locations are powerful for learning math at all levels, including algebra, geometry, even calculus.

As the old saying goes, "If you give a man a fish, you feed him for a day. If you teach a man to fish, you feed him for a lifetime." It is my hope that this framework will allow you to generate your own collection of math possibilities spurred on by the examples that I've presented. I invite you to celebrate the explosion of math opportunities on the following pages. Remember, it's not about math, it's about life.

A GROCERY STORE

Whether your grocery store shopping experiences stem from going to the general store in town once a week or shopping at a "marketplace" store on a daily basis, you encounter hundreds of math application opportunities in the process. Regardless of your age, geographical location, or profession, going to the grocery store is a necessity for us all. As rich in math potential for students as for consumers, a behind-the-scenes look is truly fascinating for young and old alike.

Significant Information About the Location

This particular store, one of a large chain, is new and is considered a "marketplace" because it offers a greater variety of customer services than an average grocery store. Located in this store is a deli, bakery, pharmacy, florist, snack bar, and fish market. This store averages 650 customers through its doors daily and is open from 6:00 a.m. to 12:00 p.m., 363 days per year. The store employs 140 full-time and part-time employees. A part-time employee averages approximately 20 hours per week. Each department of the store has its own manager; there is also a head manager who oversees the entire operation.

General questions to pose for further study of your local grocery store

- Does your family shop at the same store that you visited with your class? If not, how is your store the same or different?

- How many years has your store been in operation?

- Is your store part of a national or regional chain or is it independently operated?

- How many people are employed by your store? Full-time? Part-time?

- What is the average number of customers that your grocery store serves on a daily basis?

- How many grocery stores are within 1, 3, 5, or 10 miles of your store? What effect do you think this has on your store?

"Do what you can, with what you have, where you are."

Theodore Roosevelt

Financial Aspects

The grocery industry receives its revenues from the sale of groceries and from companies that pay them for advertising. The costs of running a grocery store are extremely high, the average profit margin for most stores being very small, 1%-5%. Yet high sales volume makes a worthwhile profit even on this small margin. Because large chains possess more buying power (thus lower purchase prices), it is very difficult for a local, independent store to compete.

In the grocery industry, 8%-11% of all revenues are allocated to salaries. Salaries of grocery store employees range from a bagger making $5.25 per hour to a pharmacist who can begin at $27.25 per hour. Managers work on annual salaries as opposed to hourly wages.

A major cost of most grocery stores is advertising. These costs are incurred by producing television ads, radio spots, newspaper ads, and coupon booklets.

Questions to pose regarding the financial aspects of a grocery store

- How many employees does the store employ? What is the percentage of full-time to part-time employees?

- What are the sources of income for the store?

- How much of the store's budget do salaries represent? Do you think this is fair? Why or why not?

- What is the annual cost of advertising for your store? How are these costs broken down (radio, TV, newspaper, etc.)? Can you think of any ways that your store could advertise without it costing more money?

- If you were responsible for grocery shopping for your family, would you shop at this store? Why or why not?

Physical Characteristics of the Location

This store is 49,000 square feet in size; 48,000 square feet for the sales floor, 1,000 square feet for office space, employee lounge, and delivery/storage areas.

During an average month, a store of this size spends approximately $20,000 on electricity, $500 on water, and $700 on phone bills. During an average year, a store of this size spends $30,000-$50,000 on daily maintenance and cleaning.

Repairs to equipment must also be accounted for. It is not unusual for a store of this size to spend $6,000-$10,000 per month on these repairs. As time goes on, older stores will expend a greater percentage of their budgets to these repairs. One of the most expensive kinds of repairs is the replacement of a compressor. Replacing one single compressor could cost as much as $10,000, not including the cost of the spoiled food.

Questions to pose regarding the physical characteristics of a grocery store

- How many square feet does the store utilize? How much of this space is open to the public? How does this size compare to the size of your classroom, your school, or your home?

- What are the operating costs per month? Per year?

- Based on the age of the store, what are the estimated costs of annual repairs?

- How much money does the store spend on basic maintenance? How does this compare to what your family spends on maintaining your house?

Inventory

Inventory related issues at a grocery store could resemble those of a revolving door. A store of this size can have as many as 40,000 items which must be stocked and restocked all day, everyday. There are two sources from which most grocery stores, affiliated with a regional or national chain, receive their merchandise: direct delivery from the supplier and from the warehouse. Items that may typically come from the warehouse may include anything from fresh produce and meat to canned goods and could total as much as 5,000 cases of merchandise per week. These items can be transported from the warehouse on a daily basis. Items coming from direct deliveries could include fresh breads, soda pop, and chips to gourmet salads and meats. All orders are communicated to the warehouse via computer.

Practical Applications

Questions to pose regarding inventory at the grocery store

- How many items does the store stock?

- How often does the store receive deliveries? How is this important?

- What are the sources of the store's inventory? Are they local?

- What happens to the produce supply if there is a frost, drought, etc?

- What are the best selling items? Do specific items sell better at certain times of the year? Why do you think this is true?

- Who decides on the prices of the items and when to have sales?

- If the store is part of a national chain, must each store order the same thing? Why or why not? Do you agree with this policy?

Daily Uses

In addition to the physical costs, salaries, advertising, and maintenance and operating costs of a grocery store, there are numerous other ways that math is used daily. Creating weekly work schedules for employees, as well as projecting upcoming needs are two additional ways math is applied. Projecting upcoming needs in a grocery store can be based on numerous factors. An upcoming holiday, Thanksgiving or Christmas, for example, will necessitate additional supplies of gravy, turkey, cranberries, or other foods we generally associate with traditional holiday meals. Special events, such as the Super Bowl, could necessitate additional supplies of chips, hot dogs, or hamburgers. Being able to accurately predict and estimate these variations could make or cost your grocery store thousands of dollars.

A strong spatial sense in terms of physical space is another crucial mathematical skill associated with the grocery industry. Estimating how many cans will fit into a particular space and how long the supply will last is another skill that is required. If the warehouse must make additional deliveries, the cost of your merchandise rises due to additional miles driven by the truck, gas required to transport the inventory, and the salary of the driver. Not being able to calculate this correctly could cost your grocery store thousands of dollars.

Creating promotional displays is another task that requires a strong spatial sense. How many items will it take to create the display? Where will the display be created? On a table? On the floor? On a crate? Will the items balance so that they don't fall over? If they fall over and break, how costly is the mistake?

Calculating coupon deductions is a task to which math is applied daily at a grocery store. Sometimes promotional events are accompanied by the store changing the value of a coupon, offering double or even triple the value, up to a certain amount. When a vendor offers a coupon for one of its products, they cover the cost of the coupon, in addition to offering the store an 8-cent handling fee. When stores double and triple the worth of a coupon, the store pays the additional difference. Store employees that accept expired coupons are a source of great loss for most grocery stores because the stores are not reimbursed for this cost.

Coupon books that are printed are usually paid for by the manufacturer(s) of the items being advertised. These costs do not come from the store itself. The manufacturer pays to have books created, assembled, and mailed. Promotional allowance from manufacturers can allow for pricing and cover some of the costs of the book. The items that appear in the various coupon books are generally keyed to the season or to a special event.

Shoplifting is a serious problem for grocery stores, often running as high as 1 to 1.5 percent of gross sales, a figure that can equal the store's profit margin.

In addition to the daily math uses for the entire store mentioned above, each department in a grocery store has its own daily math uses. The following list is an example of several departments and a sampling of their designated daily math uses:

Department	*Functions/Questions*
Deli	• Weighing meats, cheeses, salads, figuring price per pound, half-pound, etc.
	• Cooking, calculating oven temperatures and cooking time
	• Measuring, preparing different kinds of side dishes
	• What percentage of the store's total revenue comes from the deli?
Bakery	• Measuring to bake breads, cakes, pies, etc.
	• Calculating projected needs. How many more pumpkin pies will you need just before Thanksgiving as compared to mid-July?
	• How much of which ingredients must you stock to be able to bake what you need?
	• What percentage of the store's total revenue comes from the bakery?

Practical Applications

Pharmacy
- Calculating the correct dosage for each prescription

- How many pills will the customer need to take per day and how many milligrams should each pill consist of?

- What are the differences in cost between name brand drugs and their generic counterpart?

- What percentage of the store's total revenue comes from the pharmacy?

Floral
- Quantity of flowers, plants, or balloons and their profit margins

- Determining costs for specially ordered arrangements

- What percentage of the store's total revenue comes from the floral department?

Questions to pose regarding the daily uses of mathematics at the grocery store

- Which departments do the greatest or least amount of business? Which have the greatest and the least markup on average? Why?

- Are some departments busier at certain times of the day or the year? Why? What could you do to increase sales in certain departments? Why do you think this might be successful?

- How many special displays does your grocery store have at one time? What, if any, are the additional costs to create them?

- How far do the various delivery trucks travel to reach the store? How does this distance take away from or add to the store's profits? What does the current gasoline price have to do with this figure?

- How much money does your grocery store lose annually due to the acceptance of expired coupons?

- How much money does your family save per week by using coupons? If your family is not using coupons, design a system to help your family begin saving coupons. If your family is already saving coupons, create strategies to increase the use of coupons and save additional money.

Special Events

Throughout the year, grocery stores take part in numerous special events: some initiated by the store's marketing program (e.g., Grand Openings, sales leaders), some requested by the public (such as special foods for holidays, ethnic foods), and others in response to special events including campaigns for various community-based organizations and community events. For example, Safeway in Phoenix is a major sponsor for the Phoenix Cardinals and is the number one contributor to Easter Seals. Year-round donations and collections to local food banks are also encouraged.

Questions to pose regarding special events at the grocery store

- Does your local grocery store ever have special events? What are they? Have you ever participated in them?

- How much money is the grocery store able to generate from special events? Who gets this revenue?

- How much additional money does it cost the grocery store to put on a special event?

- How many people participate in the special event?

- How many times per year do special events occur? What other special events could the grocery store sponsor?

- If you were to design your own special event for your local grocery store, what would it be? Why would you choose to do it?

General Suggestions For a "Being There" Experience at the Grocery Store

Kathy Loraso, manager of a Safeway store in Scottsdale, Arizona, reports that students of all ages can enjoy a "being

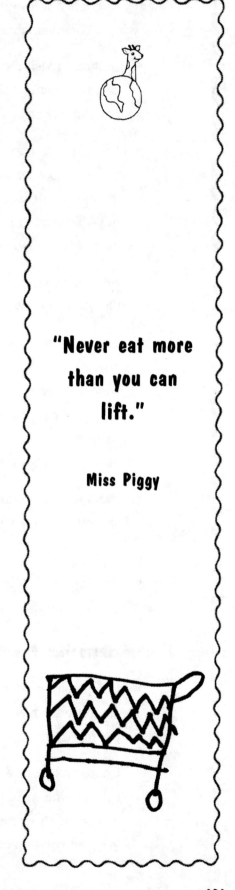

"Never eat more than you can lift."

Miss Piggy

there" experience at the grocery store. Depending on the ages of your students, I offer the following recommendations to enhance your experience:

- Be sure to visit the store location at the beginning of your study so that students can see firsthand what they will be studying; this makes the math applications real and concrete. Revisit frequently and as a culminating activity if possible.

- Bring a videotape recorder to record your experience. This way you'll have a resource to refer back to once you leave the grocery store. It is helpful to have another adult or older student handle the videotaping. This frees you to pose questions and guide your students and will likely improve the quality and usefulness of the videotape.

- Bring a camera; take pictures representing each department of the grocery store. Once they're developed you'll have a visual record of items in each department.

- Divide your class into two, three, or four study groups, based on interest. One group may want to spend their time learning about the bakery, while others may choose to learn about produce, or dry goods. Each group spends their time with an expert person from a particular department. Once you return to the classroom, each group could prepare a presentation about their department to teach the rest of the class about their area of interest.

- Provide each child with a clipboard or other hard surface to write on so that students can take notes while walking around or listening.

In addition to the opportunities proposed in each category above, the following projects can be used to extend or assess what your students know and how they can apply their knowledge.

K-3 Mathematics Possibilities from a Grocery Store Experience

- Using data gathered at the grocery store, write at least three story problems; compute the answers to all three. Choose your best story problem and give it to the rest of the class to solve. Compare their answers with yours.

- Choose a particular product (shampoo, dog food, etc.). Count and tally how many brand names your grocery store has in stock of this product. Create a poster, or pie or bar graph to show your results. Which brand is the most or least expensive? Why do you think this is so? Be prepared to show the class your results.

- Estimate how many customers will enter the store in a five-minute time period. Stand at the front door of the store. Count and tally how many customers enter in five minutes. Compare your estimate to your actual count.

- Given a specified amount of money, which cereal (or other product) would you buy for your family? Do you have a coupon for one kind and not another? How did you make your decision? Be prepared to report your findings to your family.

- Collect and sort coupons from the Sunday newspaper circular. Based on the coupons you collect, create categories (i.e., desserts, cereals, etc.) and count how many coupons are offered for each category. If you picked three items to buy, how much money would you save from the coupons you chose?

- Invite store personnel to be guest speakers to your classroom. Encourage students to interview guests to determine what kinds of experiences and schooling each person needs to be able to do their jobs. How does each person use math in their jobs on a daily basis?

4-6 Mathematics Possibilities from the Grocery Store Experience

- Collect and sort coupons from the Sunday newspaper circular. Based on your coupons, create categories (e.g., desserts, cereals, etc.) and count how many coupons are offered for each such category. Plan a weekly menu for your family. How many of the coupons could you use? How much money could this save your family for one week? Two weeks? One month? One year? Don't forget to calculate if your store is doubling or tripling the value of your coupons.

- Interview an employee from the grocery store. Find out all of the ways that the person uses math skills to do his or her job. Compare this list of skills to those you are learning in school. Write an action plan for yourself about which math skills you may need to improve if you ever wanted to work in a grocery store.

- Compare how much money the grocery store spends in a month/a year on maintenance and operations with such costs for your school or your home. Show your results in a Venn diagram or other graphic organizer.

- Calculate the amount of money needed for your trip to the grocery store. Include bus costs to get there. Record your findings and publish results for your class.

- Invite store personnel to be guest speakers to your classroom. Encourage students to interview guests to determine what kinds of experiences and schooling each

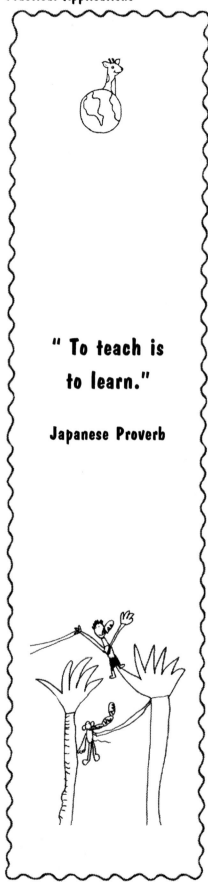

Practical Applications

" To teach is
to learn."

Japanese Proverb

person needs to be able to do their jobs. How does each person use math in their jobs on a daily basis?

- Using data gathered at the grocery store, write at least three story problems; compute the answers to all three. Choose your best story problem and give it to the rest of the class to solve. Compare their answer with yours.

As you reflect on all of the curriculum possibilities explored, you will see that the grocery store can provide a month's worth of curriculum. Once again, I have only focused on mathematics application opportunities! So, the next time you are hungry and go to the grocery store, think about how you can satisfy your hunger for real-life math application opportunities for your students as well as satisfying your own appetite!

A ZOO

A zoo, with all its exotic animals and concessions offering a range of smells and tastes, is a guaranteed kid-grabber. And, the math possibilities are endless! Although every zoo is different in the way it is run, the number of animals exhibited, its physical size, its revenues, etc., there are some basic tenets that will apply to most zoos. The Phoenix Zoo in Arizona provides a good illustration of the math possibilities inherent in zoos. [Note: In a rural area far from a zoo, apply these same questions to the operation of a nearby ranch or farm.]

Significant Information About the Location

The Phoenix Zoo opened in 1962 on 125 acres of land. At that time, approximately 25%-30% of the zoo was developed. Currently, approximately 50% of the zoo has been developed either as an exhibition or visitor service site. Approximately one million people visit the Phoenix Zoo annually. School field trips account for approximately ten percent of the one million visitors. The majority of all school visitors are five to nine years old (K-4). This zoo hosts 1,300 animals of 320 species, including 200 endangered animals from the world's most beautiful and fragile ecosystems. The Phoenix Zoo employs 145 full-time and 25 part-time people and relies on the services of more than 350 volunteers to operate. The zoo is open every day of the year except Christmas. Regular zoo hours are 9:00-5:00 with extended hours in the summer. The Phoenix Zoo is operated by a private, nonprofit organization. Other zoos in this country may be privately owned, city owned, or state owned.

General questions to pose for further study

- How many years has your zoo been in existence? What percentage of its land is developed?

- How many people visit annually? How many of these visitors are children? Why do you think this may be true?

- How many animals are at your zoo? How many are on the endangered and threatened species list?

- How many people work and volunteer at the zoo? How many staff and volunteers would be needed once the zoo is fully developed?

- If you spent two minutes viewing each animal, how many days would it take to see all of the animals?

Financial Aspects

The Phoenix Zoo operates on an annual budget of $4,000,000. The three major sources of income are: admissions, concessions, and zoo memberships. Admissions are categorized based on age and membership:

Visitor's Age	Cost
13-59	$7.00
60+	$6.00
4-12	$3.00
Under 3	FREE
Zoo Member	FREE

There are several different kinds of membership packages available. A basic membership is $35.00 annually for two adults and two children. An additional $5.00 per child is added for each child over the basic membership. A Keeper's Club membership is $125.00. The Adopt an Animal program contributes directly to the zoo's operating budget that feeds and cares for the animals managed by the zoo; it brings in approximately $100,000 in revenue annually.

The Phoenix Zoo does not receive any government monies but does lease their land from the City of Phoenix for $1.00 per year. Annual private donations from individuals and special fund-raising events finance development and improvement of exhibits and visitor amenities. Most private donations (amounts vary) are targeted by the donor for a specific purpose or a specific animal's support. Salaries for people working at the zoo range from $5.75 per hour to $19.00 per hour.

Questions to pose regarding the financial aspects of the zoo

- How much land is the zoo located on?

- How much does it cost to keep the zoo operating annually? What will be the projected cost five years from now? How do you know?

- What are the sources of income for the zoo? How would the zoo maintain itself if some of the current sources of income disappeared?

- Are there different kinds of memberships available? If so, what are the packages?

- How much of the budget do salaries represent?

- How many people work at the zoo? How many people hours does it take to run the zoo for a week?

Physical Characteristics of the Location

Each exhibit is specifically designed and targeted for a particular animal. Therefore, the cost of creating and maintaining different exhibits varies greatly. In terms of space, it is critical to examine the animals' needs and behaviors. For example, when designing a habitat for a lion, one must consider having enough space for the lion horizontally. When designing a habitat for a monkey, one must consider having enough space both horizontally and vertically so that the monkey can swing and climb. Some animals live underground. For nocturnal animals, special lighting is needed to trick the animals into thinking that their active period occurs during the day.

The Phoenix Zoo is currently creating an exhibition called, "The Forest of Uco." This exhibit will house the Uco bear and will be an immersion into the culture of the peoples of Colombia. The anticipated cost of this exhibit is $1.6 million dollars. All of this money is expected to come from private donations.

Similar types of exhibits may have very different costs depending on the weather in the area of the country they are created in. Winterizing or summerizing particular habitats may be very costly. The Phoenix Zoo spends an average of $250,000 annually just on utilities (water and electricity).

Questions to pose regarding the physical characteristics of the zoo

- How much does the zoo spend on utilities such as water, electricity, telephone? How much does it spend on basic maintenance (repairs)? Can you think of some ways to help the zoo save money on some of these basic utilities and maintenance expenditures?

- What is the average cost of designing, creating, and maintaining an exhibition? If you were going to create a special exhibit, what animal would it be for? How would you design it? What materials would you use? What would your building budget be?

- If you were going to design your own zoo, how much acreage would you need? How many animals would you begin with? Which animals would be the most cost effective to begin your zoo? Why? How many employees would you have? What hours should it be open to the public? Why?

Inventory

There are many factors to consider when thinking about the inventory of a zoo, e.g., cost of purchasing and feeding an animal, design and construction of a habitat for it, stocking and restocking the gift shop and concession stands and so forth. For example, many zoos are no longer buying animals but instead are trading them with other zoos. Costs per animal are high: a zebra may cost $10,000 and a female cheetah could cost $20,000. These costs vary from species to species and depend on status and availability. The cost of feeding all of the animals annually at the Phoenix Zoo is $175,000. In 1991, the animals at the Phoenix Zoo polished off: 32 tons of fruit, 38 tons of vegetables, 24 tons of meat, 100 tons of hay, straw, grain, and bread, and 30 gallons of milk! The average daily intake for each elephant alone at the Phoenix Zoo is: 50 gallons of water, 55 lbs. of hay, 10 pounds of potatoes, and 10 pounds of carrots!! No wonder they're so large! Interestingly enough, elephants in the wild eat even more because they are not fed such a nutritionally rich diet.

Practical Applications

The concession stands at the zoo sell approximately $1,580,000 of soda, hot dogs, and candy annually. Gift shop sales vary annually.

Questions to pose regarding inventory at the zoo

- What is the average life span of a particular animal?

- Which animal at your zoo was the most or least expensive to purchase? Why?

- How much money does the zoo spend to feed the animals weekly, monthly, annually?

- How much would it cost you per week/month/year to feed four of your favorite zoo animals?

- What is the average weekly cost to feed the animals? Compare this to feeding an average family of four.

- How much does a particular animal weigh? What is its gestation period, wing span, length, etc.?

- How does this compare to other animals of the same species? To your pet?

- Explore the anatomy and physiology of an animal, e.g., how many vertebrae does a giraffe have? (*Answer:* the same as a human; they're just designed differently.)

- How much does the gift shop sell in a week, month, or year? What are the best selling items? Why do you think some items sell better than others? Could you design a marketing plan to help sell those items not selling well now?

- How are items priced? What is the average markup per item? Is it the same for all items? Why or why not?

Daily Uses

In addition to calculating admissions, concessions, and memberships, employees at the zoo use math for computing other special fees or income such as the following:

Special Services	Cost
Special tours	$2.00 per person
Camel ride	$2.00 per person
Stroller rental	$2.00/$4.00 (single/double seat)
Wheelchair rental	$5.00

Questions to pose regarding the daily uses of mathematics at the zoo

- Do all of the concession stands sell the same amount in a day? Why or why not?

- What is the average rental rate for special services listed above? Do you think these prices are reasonable? Should they be more or less? Why?

- Which days of the year does the zoo have the most or fewest visitors. Why? If you had your own zoo, what are some strategies that you would use to try to get people to visit the zoo more consistently? Could you propose these ideas to the directors of your own local zoo?

Special Events

The Phoenix Zoo offers numerous special events annually. Some are service oriented and some are fund-raising opportunities for the zoo. Some of the special events offered include inviting classes to stay overnight at the zoo in order to provide a more in-depth exploration of nature in both diurnal and nocturnal settings. The cost of this experience is $25.00 per student. Special events for different holidays also may encourage a special event such as "Boo at the Zoo" for a Halloween themed event and "Zoolights" for the December holidays.

Questions to pose regarding special events at the zoo

- How much money is the zoo able to generate from special events? Has this changed over the past five, ten, or twenty years? Why or why not?

- How much additional money does it cost the zoo to put on a special event? Does the event pay for itself?

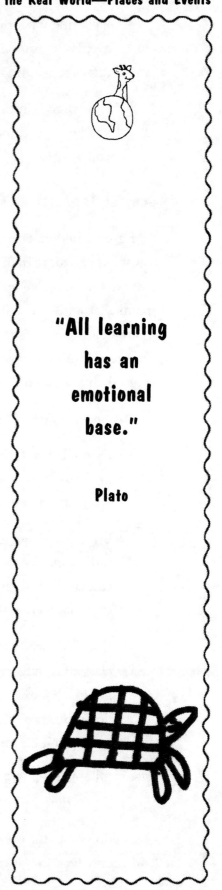

"All learning has an emotional base."

Plato

- How many people participate in the special events? What other ideas for special events do you have? What would you have to know about math in order to do this successfully?

- How many times per year do special events occur? If this were your zoo, would you hold the same special events or have different ones? If different, what would you have?

General Suggestions for a "Being There" Experience at the Zoo

Karen Schedler, Education Services Coordinator at the Phoenix Zoo, states that, "The zoo should be more than a P.E. exercise." She reports that the majority of classrooms that come to the zoo have approximately two hours to view the zoo, most of which is spent zooming around to see all the animals. Few classrooms take the time to observe and learn about a particular animal or group of animals. Learning should be more focused and in-depth; so be sure to provide adequate time for students to observe closely a few concepts rather than attempt to "cover" the potential of the zoo.

Here are Ms. Schedler's recommendations along with some of my own:

- Do not bring your child or class to the zoo only as a culminating activity. Instead, bring them toward the beginning of your study to focus and ground student observation and research.

- Bring a videotape recorder to capture your experience and create a resource to refer back to once you leave the zoo. It is helpful to have another adult or older student handle the videotaping. This frees you to pose questions and guide your students and will likely improve the quality and usefulness of the videotape.

- Instead of walking all around the zoo, have a particular point of focus. Your entire class may have the same focus or perhaps you may want to break into two groups. For example: one group may spend their entire time on the Arizona Trail, becoming experts on specific snakes or Gila monsters, while another group may spend their entire time becoming experts on a particular bird or reptile.

- Provide each child with a clipboard or other hard surface to write on. This way the student can take notes while walking around or listening to a speaker.

In addition to the opportunities proposed in each category, the following projects will lend themselves to assessing what your students know and how they can apply their knowledge. Remember, if you are implementing the ITI Model, connect these inquiry choices directly to your key points. For more information, please refer to *ITI: The Model* by Susan Kovalik with Karen Olsen.

K-3 Mathematics Possibilities From Zoo Experience

- Using data gathered at the zoo, write at least three story problems; compute the answers to all three. Choose your best story problem and give it to the rest of the class to solve. Compare their answer with yours.

- Observe and record the activity of an animal for a given period of time. You may write or draw pictures of what you observed. In a five-minute period, what was the animal doing and for how many times? Be prepared to share your observations with the class by creating a graph or poster. Were your findings greater or less than you may have anticipated?

- Create a Venn diagram comparing two animals that you observed by characteristics (2-legged, 4 -legged, tails, etc.). Be sure to include at least six different attributes. Share your findings with one of your classmates.

- Calculate the amount of money needed for a field trip for your family or your learning club (small group). Be sure to include admission and bus costs. Record your calculations and budget on a piece of paper or a poster and share them with your class.

- Record and compare the different types and amounts eaten by specific animals. Include at least two different foods the animal eats. Illustrate your results using a pie or bar graph.

- Build a model of a habitat for a specific animal. Clay, popsicle sticks, or any other material may be used. As you build, generate a list of directions so it can be recreated by another person. When you write your directions, be sure to include: how many, how much, how big, etc. You may want to have an older "buddy" scribe for you as you dictate your directions.

- Tally how many animals you saw that have two legs, four legs, no legs. Graph your results.

"Sooner or later, every generation must find its voice."

Henry Louis Gates, Jr.

4-6 Mathematics Possibilities From Zoo Experience

• Create a timeline to show the history of the zoo. Include indicators to show when different exhibitions were added or deleted, when specific animals were added, moved, born in captivity, or died. Include projections (both already planned projections along with a few of your own ideas) for the development in the zoo for the next twenty years.

• Create a bar graph, line graph, or pie chart to illustrate the different demographics of the people who visit the zoo annually. Include gender, age, and other factors you think important to tell the story of the people who come. Compare these demographics to those in your city. Be ready to present these results to the people in the marketing department at the zoo with a plan of how to increase visitation by underrepresented groups.

• Make a poster showing the ratio of zoo animals that are endangered animals vs. those that are not. What can we do to help those in our area that may be endangered? Research and formulate a plan including at least three steps.

• Measure the space of the habitat of the animal you are studying. Create a model of it to scale. If the zoo is preparing for a new exhibit, design and construct a 3-D model of a habitat for the animal. Be prepared to explain why you designed it as you did.

• Design and produce a one-to-three page flyer for the zoo describing all of the different membership packages available to potential zoo members. Be sure to include who and how many people are included, membership benefits, and costs. Present the flyer to the staff at the zoo as a potential marketing strategy.

- Compare how much money the zoo spends annually on maintenance and operations with such expenses for your school. Show your results in a Venn diagram, or other graphic organizer. Be sure to include at least four categories of maintenance and operations.

- Compare the amount and cost of weekly intake of food for one animal; compare it to that of your family. Illustrate results using a pie chart, bar graph, or line graph.

- Using data gathered at the zoo, write at least three story problems; compute the answers to all three. Choose your best story problem and give it to the rest of the class to solve. Compare their answers with yours.

- Observe and record the activity of an animal for a given period of time. You may write or draw pictures of what you observed. In a five-minute period, what was the animal doing and for how many times? Be prepared to share your observations to the class by creating a graph or poster.

As you can plainly see, an in-depth study of the zoo itself, not to mention in-depth studies of the animals, can provide an enormous amount of math curriculum for your students. You may have already thought of many of your own ideas to add to the possibilities above. So, the next time you're thinking about a rich experience for your students, remember to "do the zoo!"

AN AIRPORT

As a "being there" experience, a visit to an airport is another guaranteed kid-grabber. Planes taking off and landing, luggage carousels and trains, air traffic control centers . . . irresistible! Whether the student has actually flown or not is immaterial. Airports are amazing places. Whether you live in a major metropolitan area or out in rural countryside, you're probably not too far from an airport of some size. To help us explore the math opportunities associated with an airport, I am using Sky Harbor International Airport, located in Phoenix, Arizona, as an example.

The numbers associated with an airport are unlimited and huge. This is a time for students to marvel at how big things can be! For very young children, big numbers are not developmentally appropriate but there are still lots of kid-sized issues to deal with. So, whatever their ages, enjoy!

Significant Information About the Location

Sky Harbor International Airport's history begins in 1928 when Scenic Airways bought 278 acres in Phoenix to begin an airport. In 1935, the City of Phoenix purchased the airport for $100,000. At that time, Sky Harbor was known as "The Farm" because their single unpaved runway also doubled as a pasture. Today the airport sits on 2,232 acres of land and includes four terminals (three for passengers). It is currently the eighth busiest airport in the United States for passenger traffic and is the eighteenth busiest airport in the world, serving 25 million people annually. International passenger arrivals increased more than 90% in 1995. Over the past ten years, air traffic has grown from 11.0 million passengers a year to more than 26.7 million, a 142% increase. The total number of people employed directly on the airport property in 1995 was 21,373; the payroll exceeded $627 million. In addition to Sky Harbor the City of Phoenix also owns two nearby "sister" airports.

General questions to pose for further study

- Have you ever been to your local airport? What did you do there?

- Which other airports, if any, have you been to?

- What do you remember about your airport experience?

- Which U.S. airports are busier than Sky Harbor? How large are the cities they serve?

- Do you think Sky Harbor could ever become one of the top five busiest U.S. airports? Why or why not?

- There is now speculation about the need for an additional third runway. How is that decided and who makes that decision? What would a third runway cost?

- How many more terminals could be built on the airport property if needed? How much busier does the airport have to be to consider a new terminal?

- How many airlines use Sky Harbor International Airport?

- How many people are in your school? How many of your "schools" would it take to equal the number of people who work at the airport?

Financial Aspects

Sky Harbor, owned by the City of Phoenix, is a self-sustaining department; no tax revenue is needed to help run it. During fiscal year 1995, Sky Harbor and its two sister airports made economic contributions to the Greater Phoenix metropolitan area of more than $37 million a day and over $13 billion annually. According to industry experts, "the economic impact of the Phoenix Airport System on the economy of the Valley of the Sun will double in the next 10 years, growing from the current $13.5 billion to more than $22 billion in 2005. The average daily economic value of each arriving or departing aircraft is $33,514." Income sources "include rent from tenants such as airlines, auto rental agencies, concessions, restaurants, and aircraft sales/maintenance shops. Other revenue sources include parking fees, aviation fuel sales, and hangar rentals. Even grants received from the federal government and the State of Arizona come from aviation user fees and not taxes from the general public. In short, the Phoenix Airport System pays its own way. It is a proven community asset which generates millions of dollars of economic activity daily and does so at no cost to the taxpayer."[1] The following pie graphs represent the sources and uses of revenue for fiscal year 1995.[2]

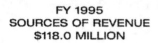

FY 1995
SOURCES OF REVENUE
$118.0 MILLION

FY 1995
USES OF REVENUE
$118.0 MILLION

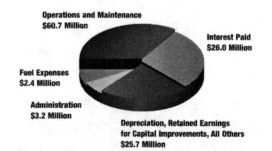

When looking at the above graphs, it is easy to see that parking fees and auto rental agencies represent the second largest source of revenue. These parking fees are most likely the source of revenue that we, the public, may be most familiar with. In fact, there are approximately 12,442 daily parking transactions. Parking rates at the airport are as follows:

.80¢ per half hour

$11.00 daily maximum at Terminals 3 & 4

$5.50 daily maximum at Terminal 2

Questions to pose regarding the financial structure of the airport

- Which source of revenue represents the greatest source of revenue for the airport? How much does it represent?

- Do fuel sales represent more or less revenue than landing and terminal fees?

Practical Applications

- If the average daily economic value of each arriving or departing aircraft is $33,514, how much revenue would be generated in two days? Three days? One week? One month?

- Looking at the pie graphs for uses of revenue, do fuel expenses represent a large percentage of the total uses or a small percentage? How much more money is used for administrative costs than for fuel?

- What are the costs of running your classroom (supplies), or your school? How do these compare to the costs of running Sky Harbor Airport?

- How much would it cost to park your car at the airport for one hour? Two hours? Eight hours?

- If you were going on a trip for one week and had to park your car at the airport, how much would it cost if you parked in Terminal 2? Terminal 3? What is the difference in cost? Why do you think there is a difference in cost?

Physical Characteristics of the Location

Sky Harbor International Airport is located near the center of the state; it is just 6 miles/10 km or 13 minutes by car from downtown Phoenix and the state capitol. There are 100 gates located throughout the three passenger terminals of Sky Harbor. The three passenger terminals take up 2,947,421 total square feet. A $27.7 million expansion project recently completed at Terminal 4 added eight new gate positions for Southwest Airlines and two additional international gates. A total of 9,850 public parking spaces are available. Currently, there are two runways at Sky Harbor; one measures 11,000 feet and the other measures 10,300 feet. Electric bills for the airport cost approximately $338,400 annually. Water to maintain the grounds alone costs the airport $556,829 annually.

Questions to pose regarding the physical characteristics of the airport

- Where is the nearest airport in your city or state? (Near the center of town? Northeast corner? Two hours south, etc.?) How many miles/km is the airport from your house? Why do you think your airport was built in its present location?

- How many gates does your airport have? How many different airlines are served by each gate? Do different airlines share gates?

- How many runways does your airport have? How long are they? What would that look like if you measured the same distance in your neighborhood?

Inventory

Sky Harbor Airport serves 20 different passenger carriers such as American, America West, Delta, United, and TWA, as well as freight carriers such as Federal Express, United Parcel Service, and the U.S. Postal Service. It acts as a major operational "hub" for America West Airlines and Southwest Airlines. The "hub" serves as a connection site for all flights. This means that these airlines have more gates than a non-hub airline, therefore, they generate more income for the airport. Training facilities for these airlines also generate more rent.

Questions to pose regarding the inventory of the airport

- How many airlines service your airport?

- How many people work at your airport? What kinds of jobs are available there? Would you want to have any of the jobs mentioned above? Why or why not?

- Is your local airport a training site for a given airline? If so, does the airport generate more money from them? How?

- Do commercial passenger airlines make as much money as parcel carriers? Why or why not?

Daily Uses

Sky Harbor was ranked among the highest on-time airports in the United States in 1995. It also has the highest percentage of operational time of any major airport in the United States, operating more than 95% of the time. That is pretty incredible when you consider that there are 1,111 commercial flights daily.

In 1995, there were 514,829 take-offs and landings. Approximately 70,000 people use the airport each day and

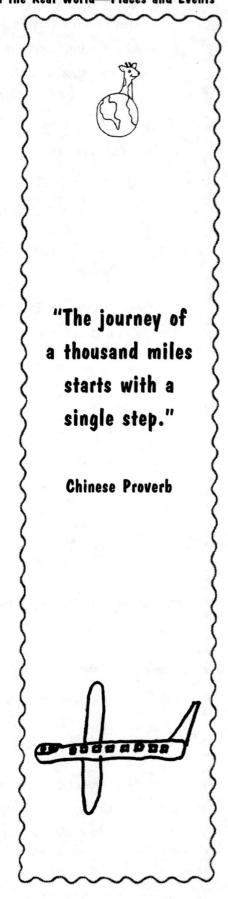

"The journey of a thousand miles starts with a single step."

Chinese Proverb

the number of travelers jumps up to approximately 105,000 for Thanksgiving! The numbers bulge during other holidays as well. On average, each person carries one to two pieces of luggage adding up to 286,666 tons of cargo in 1995. That works out to be approximately 700 tons of cargo per day. Cargo facilities include three cargo buildings totaling 197,810 square feet of space.

Traveler's services

- Shopping for everything from newspapers and sports team items to southwestern gifts, fine Native American arts, crafts, and jewelry

- Food and beverage service (Mexican food, pizza, hamburgers, snacks, etc.) 24 hours a day

- Automatic Teller Machines and a Bank One branch for banking needs right at the airport!

- Passenger Service Center for travel insurance, money orders, foreign money exchange, copy service, postage, and more

- Information Counters with ample literature on accommodations, transportation, and local attractions

- Barber shop and shoe shine services

- Rental cars

- VIP Clubs for frequent travelers

Parking and transportation

- Interterminal transportation by 35-passenger buses provides transportation between terminals every five minutes

- Taxi service by three taxi companies that serve Sky Harbor; the fare for the first mile is $2.00, each additional mile is $1.30, plus a $1.00 airport surcharge. (Total surcharge revenue paid by the taxi companies to the airport annually is $391,000.)

- Limousine service by 14 limousine companies. Charges depend on distance driven and how many passengers are included; passengers can also lease the limousine for an hourly rate of $30 per hour with a two-hour minimum charge.

Questions to pose regarding the daily uses of the airport

- On the average, how many travelers use your airport in a day, a month, a year?

- On the average, how many arrivals and departures occur in one day, one week, one month, one year? Has this rate increased or decreased in the past ten years? Why or why not?

- What are the services that your airport provides for its travelers (shops, shoe shine, taxi/limousine, food, etc.)?

- What is the increase in travel during holidays and special events, etc.?

- How many pounds of cargo are shipped from your airport daily, weekly, monthly, annually? What would these quantities look like if you tried to transport them in your family car?

- If you were going to have lunch at the airport, where would you choose to eat? How much would it cost? Sometimes airports have national chain restaurants in their facilities such as Burger King. If you purchased a meal at the Burger King at your airport, would it be the same price as the Burger King in your neighborhood? If not, why not?

- How do the different ground transportation companies solicit business? How do they compete with each other?

Special Events

Sky Harbor showcases permanent and changing fine art exhibitions and is considered the largest airport art program in the United States. It hosts three major themed exhibits each year and has more than 120 exhibits mounted.

Special events occurring in a city can have a huge effect on an airport. For example, when Superbowl XXX came to Tempe last year, the airport planned for the event for an entire year to be sure that there would be enough space for all of the commercial, charter, and private carriers that were expected. There are many such special events that could mean additional air travel to your city as well, e.g., business conventions, a musical event, community-sponsored events, sporting events.

"Every single problem that you have in your life is the seed of an opportunity for some greater belief."

Deepak Chopra

Questions to pose regarding special events at the airport

- What are possible events in your town that could mean more airplanes coming to your local airport?

- Have you ever flown to another city to do something special? Where did you go? How long did it take you to get there? How many miles from home did you go?

- How long would it have taken your family to drive there instead? What would the difference be in time and money?

General Suggestions for a "Being There" Experience at the Airport

- Do not bring your child or class to the airport only as a culminating activity. Instead, bring them toward the beginning of your study to focus and ground student observation and research.

- Bring a videotape recorder to record your experience and create a resource to refer back to once you leave the airport. It is helpful to have another adult or older student handle the videotaping. This frees you to pose questions and guide your students and will likely improve the quality and usefulness of the videotape.

- Bring a camera to take pictures representing each area of the airport. Once developed, you will have a visual record that will reactivate student memories of the visit.

- Provide each child with a clipboard or other hard surface to write on. This way the student can take notes while walking around or listening to a speaker.

- Observe the ticket counter. Pay close attention to how travelers pay for tickets. Are they using cash? credit cards? coupons?

- Walk through some of the shops at your airport. What kinds of things are for sale? Do the shops cater to tourists? Do you think items sell for the same prices as you could buy them at your local store (e.g., bottles of water, gum, etc.)? Why do you think your answer is correct?

- Observe the area where arrival and departure times are listed. How are travelers kept up-to-date about departure and arrival times, gate changes, and different flight numbers?

Other possible experiences (depending on security procedures at your local airport)

- If possible, arrange in advance for your students to board an aircraft. They can experience what it is like to be on board, buckle up, listen to safety procedures, and even be served a snack! For many students, this may be their first time actually on an airplane!

- While on the aircraft, observe the cockpit. If possible, arrange to have a pilot or other knowledgeable person tell about some of the procedures that the pilots follow when flying a plane.

- Show students the galley of the plane. Observe how food is stored and/or prepared. What shape are the food containters? Does the shape have an effect on how many food containers can be stored? Why do you think this is important?

- Observe how the baggage is transported from the ticket counter to the airplanes when departing and from the airplane to the baggage claim area when arriving at one's destination. One kindergarten teacher that I know had her students pretend to be luggage. They were actually "tagged" and were physically routed through the baggage procedures.

In addition to the opportunities proposed in each category, the following projects may lend themselves to assessing what your students know and how they can apply their knowledge.

K-3 Mathematics Possibilities From an Airport Experience

- Create your own paper airplanes either by tracing a design or creating your own. Estimate how far it can "fly" and then give it a test flight. Measure how far your airplane flew and compare it to your estimate. Record results. (For young children who may not yet know how to measure with a ruler, you may want to begin with yarn or other means of determining distance.)

- Bring in any toy airplanes you may have at home. Students can "rank" all of the airplanes; smallest to largest, thinnest to widest, lowest to highest, shortest to longest wingspan, etc. Draw a picture of your favorite "ranking."

- Using toy airplanes, blocks, and other realia, create your own airport in your classroom. Be sure to include each area that you observed on your airport study trip: ticket counter, baggage claim area, runways, shops, etc. Be sure you provide enough space between them. For example, you might not want to have the baggage claim area next to the runway, etc.

- Role-play scenarios between a ticket agent and a passenger. Determine costs of tickets to desired destinations. Then, using play money, dramatize the purchasing of the ticket(s), making change, and staying on a budget.

- Gather data from arrival/departure screens at the airport. How many flights are arriving/departing from a given airline in one day? Choose one, two, or three flights. Calculate how many hours the plane will be in the air.

- Estimate how many people will enter one of the airport exits in a five-minute time period. Stand at the exit. Count and tally how many travelers enter in five minutes. Compare your estimate to your actual count.

- Invite airline personnel to be guest speakers to your classroom. Encourage students to interview guests to determine what kinds of experiences and schooling each person needs to be able to do their jobs. How does each person use math in their jobs on a daily basis?

- Using data gathered at the airport, write at least three story problems; compute the answers to all three. Choose your best story problem and give it to the rest of the class to solve. Compare their answers with yours.

4-6 Mathematics Possibilities from an Airport Experience

- Create your own paper airplanes either by tracing a design or creating your own. Estimate how far it can "fly" and then give it a test flight. Measure how far your airplane flew and compare it to your estimate. Record results.

- Create a timeline to show the history of the airport. Include indicators to show when different terminals, shops, parking areas, etc., were added. Include projections (those already planned by airport staff along with a few of your own ideas) of future development for your airport for the next twenty years.

- Compare how much money the airline spends annually on fuel for one aircraft to the fuel bill for your family car(s). Graph your results.

- Develop your own mock airline company. Design what your planes might look like and areas of the world they would service. Figure ticket costs, employee salaries, advertising budget and means of advertising (radio, newspaper ads, TV, etc.). Design a one to three-page brochure explaining this information to potential travelers.

- Divide your group, half at one entrance, half at another. Estimate how many travelers will enter each of the two airport entrances in a five-minute time period. Count and tally how many travelers actually enter in five minutes. Compare your tallies from each entrance to your original estimates.

- Invite airline personnel to be guest speakers to your classroom. Encourage students to interview guests to determine what kinds of experiences and schooling each person needs to be able to do their jobs. How does each person use math in their jobs on a daily basis?

- What is the average number of passengers on a plane? What is the average number of flights that take off each hour? Compute the average number of people that fly each day from your airport. Do some research to find out how this compares to other airports in your region, elsewhere in the country or the world. Chart or graph your results on a poster.

- Using data gained from visiting the airport, write at least three story problems and calculate the answers to all three. Choose your best story problem and give it to the rest of the class to solve.

The next time you travel to an airport, look at it with new eyes. What are the potential curriculum opportunities that may be unique to your local airport? How are mathematical concepts used on a daily basis? How could you provide your students with a rich well of knowledge that will take them "up, up, and away" with practical math application experiences? Have a nice flight!

Using the examples of a grocery store, a zoo, and an airport, I have given you a framework to view any study trip experience to help your students "find the math." Hopefully, they will begin to "see the math" in places you yourself may not have immediately recognized. By doing so, you will be giving your students the gift of understanding how math is used in the real world in real situations. Once you apply this framework to your own local place of study, mathematical application possibilities will be limitless, meaningful, and relevant! And your students' math achievements will soar.

Keep in mind: "Learning in mathematics is synonymous with doing—predicting and verifying, generalizing, finding and expressing patterns, modeling, visualizing, conjecturing, linking ideas. This "doing" is done not by the teacher but by the student."[3]

For Further Study

Local Yellow Pages!
The Internet

Chapter 11
Practical Applications:

Micro-Communities—
Reality-Based Community
Simulations

Creating a micro-community within your educational setting is a rich and exciting way to actively engage students in real-life problem solving. A micro-community can be created at various levels: schoolwide, within one "house" or grade level, or even in an individual classroom. This chapter takes a look at each of these situations. We begin by focusing on the schoolwide micro-community created by Jacobson Elementary, Las Vegas, Nevada, called Jacobsonville with an in-school currency known as "Bear Bucks."

A SCHOOLWIDE MICRO-COMMUNITY

The ideal situation is obviously a schoolwide micro-community which, due to its size, can be the most complex and thus lifelike. From students' perspective, there is no gap to jump between school and working in the micro-community—they are one and the same. From the teachers' perspective, there are many heads and hands to share the work; each person's load is light in comparison to the payback.

The most real, lifelike, rich, and complex micro-community I know of is Jacobsonville, at Walter E. Jacobson Elementary, a K-5 school. Year round and five track, it is integrated into teachers' classroom themes and is a daily occurrence. With daily postal service, stores to shop, and businesses (individual and class) to run, weekly court sessions, and annual city elections, it is the engine that drives students' enthusiasm for learning a wide range of basic skills and content.

"Enjoyment is not the goal of education, it is the by-product of good teaching."

Dr. Lillian Katz

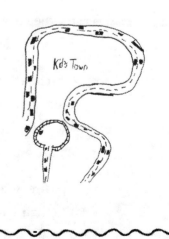

Jacobsonville As Described by Its Citizens

"Imagine an elementary school in which students learn about economics by starting their own businesses in a marketplace teaming with excitement and plenty of reading, writing, math, and practical problem solving. Imagine an educational community that prepares students to become responsible, concerned, contributing members of society. Imagine a school filled with self-assured, motivated students who are not just spectators but who are actively involved in their education.

Welcome to Jacobsonville, where a day in school is just like any other day in the real world, except here, kids run the show! Jacobsonville is a reality-based community simulation for elementary school-aged children, designed to prepare students to meet the challenges of a rapidly changing world. In Jacobsonville, students actively operate a small city which has its own government agencies and business. Here, you'll see students applying the skills they've learned in real, lifelike situations, reinforcing the fundamentals through natural learning processes.

A day in the life of Jacobsonville. Jacobsonville is a year round experience, not a special, one time only event. Here are several scenarios:

- A second grader goes to the bank to make a deposit of Bear Bucks into her interest bearing bank account. Two fourth graders are also at the bank, applying for a small business loan of thirty Bear Bucks to start their own business.

- At a Town Hall meeting, a representative reports that her district recommends the students follow a schedule to clean up the school community on a daily basis.

- During a court session, a student pleads "not guilty" to a citation received for shaking a newly planted tree. The court clerk, a fifth-grader, sets a court date; a court appointed attorney is assigned to the defendant. Meanwhile, the district attorney begins looking for witnesses for the prosecution and preparing questions to ask the defendant.

- A prospective entrepreneur attends business classes and fills out the paperwork to get a business license so she can operate legally. She pays five dollars in Bear Bucks for her business license at the city manager's office and begins to manufacture a product to be sold during Going to Town Day.

- Two first grade postal workers collect the mail from all of the classrooms and take it to their co-workers at the post office, who will stamp and sort each letter, then send it back out for same-day delivery.

- At a city council meeting, the city treasurer suggests that Jacobsonville citizens make Valentine's Day gifts to be given to residents of a local convalescent home.

- A third grade class opens its doors to a long line of citizens anxious to recycle their plastic grocery bags and aluminum cans for Bear Bucks.

- A fourth grade reporter from the Jacobsonville newspaper interviews fellow citizens for the opinion page of the monthly newspaper. On the Jacobsonville TV station, a fifth grade anchorman reports the news and introduces a commercial for the Slurpee Store at the Marketplace.

- A student attends classes in babysitting, sign language, and self defense at the University of Jacobsonville.

- The leasing office teller looks out at the long line of Jacobsonville citizens waiting to arrange to lease a booth at the Marketplace to sell their wares.

- On Going to Town Day, a young entrepreneur paints a citizen's fingernails for just three Bear Bucks. Another bargains with a customer over the price of a baseball card. A kindergartner exclaims over his purchase of homemade cookies and lemonade. A roving photographer offers to take a picture of two best friends for only five Bear Bucks. The owner of a stationery shop replenishes her stock at the booth in the Marketplace.

- A pair of entrepreneurs count their income from Going to Town Day, fill out a profit and loss statement, and split up the profit from their business.

- A kindergartner sinks down on a chair, counting his remaining Bear Bucks and sighs, 'I'm exhausted!'

As you can see, Jacobsonville citizens are learning and applying skills they will use for the rest of their lives. Their experiences in the Marketplace will have an impact on them for years to come."[1]

This micro-community is truly the ultimate immersion experience! Students are given not only mathematical application opportunities but application opportunities on how to function in a society are fostered daily! Students experience what it is like to be a functioning member of society, with all of its responsibilities, successes, and sometimes frustrations, each and every day. Such experiences add reality and meaningful context to all that they study—basic skills as well as subject content.

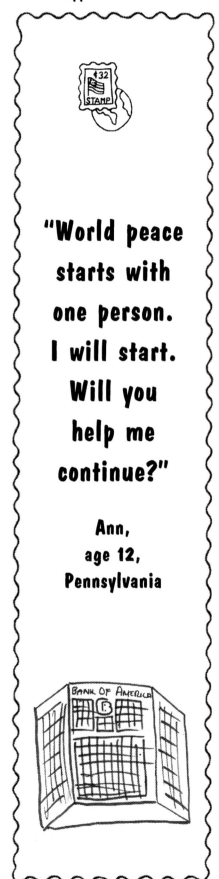

"World peace starts with one person. I will start. Will you help me continue?"

Ann,
age 12,
Pennsylvania

The scenario above is based on the model developed by Walter E. Jacobson Elementary School in Las Vegas, Nevada. For more information, contact Jacobson Elementary School in Las Vegas, Nevada, 702/799-4320. A 30-minute video about Jacobsonville is available through Books for Educators: 253/630-6908; e-mail books4@oz.net; or www. books4educ.com/

A MICRO-COMMUNITY IN A "HOUSE" SETTING

Perhaps you are interested in the creation of a micro-community at your school but do not have the buy-in from your entire staff. Many educators have developed a micro-community with a team of teachers—either by grade level or by a multi-grade span of cooperating teachers.

Micro-communities can be successful at the secondary level as well. Mohave Middle School, located in Scottsdale, Arizona, like many middle schools, operates on the "house" concept. A house consists of one hundred and sixty-five students and their five teachers. Sharing the same students allows teachers and students to build deeper relationships as they have less people to interact with on a daily basis. In 1992, "House 4" decided to create a mini-society within their own house. This simulated community involved four homeroom teachers, two alternating teachers, and the school nurse. While involving the school nurse may seem unusual, it allowed for an uncommon range of real-life opportunities as we will explore later in this chapter.

Although the team begins with a framework in mind, they readily adjust as they go based on the students. Thus, each year the micro-community has differed in significant ways from the prior year.

Students begin the semester by applying for a job at school. There are enough jobs so that each student has a specific job. Some of the job titles include: bankers, recreational leaders, landscapers, health assistants, health insurance salesperson's, and community service representatives. Each child fills out an application for his or her job and then goes through an interviewing process. Interview teams are composed of other teachers, school administrators, and parent volunteers. The "how tos" of completing a job application, resume writing, interviewing techniques, writing checks, and balancing a checkbook are part of the curriculum being presented during class time.

Students are paid minimum wage "on paper." All transactions are done via the student's checkbook. No real cash changes hands and costs vary from year to year. Students are charged fines for violating the rules. If a student gets into trouble and goes "in the red" by running out of money, he or she sometimes borrows from a friend, for little or no interest. Any student "in the red" can be held back from participating in a special privilege. The teachers report that this only happened twice in all of the years they have done this.

As in real life, students also had to pay "rent," in this case for their chair and utilities. For example, students pay $2.00 for electricity and $5.00 to make a phone call.

Going to the nurse's office requires more than simply getting a pass to do so. At the beginning of the year, the nurse teaches the students about health insurance. Three "plans" are available to the students:

Plan 1: Students may opt not to buy health insurance. If this plan is selected, a visit to the nurse's office doubles in costs.

Plan 2: The student's first visit to the nurse is "full price" but is followed by a 90/10 plan following the first visit (insurance covers 90 percent, student pays 10 percent).

Plan 3: Students pay 40% of the cost of the visits with 60% "covered" by insurance.

Before or after school and at lunch time the nurse's office becomes a "free clinic." If students are truly sick and can't pay, they are never turned away; the nurse would simply "bill" them later. Students having to take medicine or receive medical treatment on a daily basis are not penalized monetarily for their visit. But, if the nurse has to go looking for them to remind them to take their medicine, she charges them $30.00 for her time.

You may be wondering what the parents thought of this arrangement. Before the process began, these ideas were explained carefully to the parents and to the students. Feedback from both the parents and the students has all been positive. The nurse reported that many students and parents made the connections to real life. One parent stated that her daughter finally figured out why her mother wouldn't take her to the doctor for every little thing. "Now I get it when my mom tells me she can't afford to take me to the doctor."

Even though it was only paper money, students wouldn't spend their money on useless things. One student took out health insurance the prior year and never used it. So, the following year, he decided to save the money and not take out the insurance. As in real life, the following year was not identical to the previous and the student required numerous visits to the nurse and spent much more money than he would have if he would have insured himself. At midyear the student reported to the nurse, "I guess that is why they call it insurance."

Once the community jobs and businesses within the micro-community are over, every student may take part in a real business, either as a group or individually. All businesses must be approved by the principal. Types of businesses range from designing, creating, and marketing Christmas cards or greeting cards to running a jewelry business to recycling. One year, two girls operated a singing telegram business (charge, $2.00 per song!); five students put on a play and charged admission! There is always one person in a group business that takes care of up-front money and everyone makes sure that all money gets paid back. Most businesses recover their costs.

All monies funnel through a school account which is monitored by the librarian assistant and a parent. Everything is kept track of. "Bankers" use the Quicken bookkeeping software to keep track of money and prepare monthly statements. All students balance their checkbooks in their math classes. "Payroll people" work with the nurse and attendance clerk to keep track of days of school missed.

The team of teachers that orchestrate this micro-community report that their success is largely due to the commitment of other adults within the school community. The students become more self-sufficient and learn what they could do on their own, what is a necessity, and what isn't. The teachers believe that the greatest lessons of all are in students beginning to make decisions and think for themselves.

A MICRO-COMMUNITY IN ONE CLASSROOM

As mentioned earlier, a micro-community can also be accomplished in an individual classroom setting. Jennifer Salsman, a third grade teacher in Indiana, has done just that. She refers to her micro-community as an "educonomy." Jennifer states that, "We constantly make economic decisions that affect ourselves and society. This curriculum will help all children learn basic economic concepts and decision-making skills."

Each student in the classroom is expected to interview and hold a class job such as horticulturist (taking care of the plants), postmaster (putting papers in their take-home files), accountant (counts out the money each week for the salaries), banker (collects fines, keeps bank organized), sheriff (keeps our room "safe" by keeping book bags and coats off the floor, reminding students about leaning back in their chairs, etc.), office liaison (takes messages to the office), librarian (collects books on library day and returns to the library those books checked out by the teacher for classroom use).

Students are "paid" for work in "Salsman Dollars" or "WILD" money, since their theme is "Where The Wild Things Are." Students can then use their salaries to pay classroom taxes, pay a "desk mortgage" (rental) on a weekly basis, and possibly purchase items at the class store on a biweekly basis. Guest speakers from the community working in the areas of insurance, banking, and retail sales are invited to speak and answer questions.

Two different types of optional insurance are available including health and disaster, costing each student one dollar per week. Students have the option of taking out a policy each Monday. If the school has a fire or tornado drill and the student has "disaster coverage," he or she is "covered" and does not have to pay. But, if the student does not have insurance, he or she has to pay five dollars to the "insurance agent." Health insurance works the same way. If insurance is not purchased and a student is absent or visits the school nurse, he or she must pay five dollars per day. Even if the absence is an excused one, the concept is the same because another student must do the job of the absentee.

Some of the other curriculum choices include preparing and sticking to a budget, using coupons from grocery ads to plan a menu, and deciding which community service is the most important and having to explain why. The creation of an "Educonomy" in your classroom provides practical hands on experience which cannot be learned from a textbook. Students must be able to count money as they purchase insurance, pay taxes, pay desk mortgages, or shop at the class store. Every facet of the micro-community requires knowledge and involvement of economic principles.

WHY A MICRO-COMMUNITY?

Providing experiences in school that mirror real life are crucial to students' understanding of and ability to function in the real world. The creation of a micro-community, either whole school, partial school population, or even individual classroom, gives children the opportunity to interact with mathematical concepts in a real and natural way. They also help students understand how much more effective their decision making can be when they use mathematical concepts to identify, analyze, and represent the relevant data in ways that allow one to then attach value judgments in accordance with personal goals and desires. The richer and more lifelike the micro-community, the more powerful the impact on learning. Jacobson School, a year round, schoolwide micro-community, reports math tests scores of 20-30 percentile points above expected achievement levels. Application in real-life situations is key to developing mastery.

Remember, it's not about math; it's about life!

For Further Study

Jacobsonville: An ITI Microsociety (video)

Chapter 12
Practical Applications:
Daily Math Opportunities in the Classroom and School

As stated in the introduction of this book, math is everywhere—whether we are at the grocery store, the gas station, the movie theater, our living room, or even, yes, the classroom! Whether we recognize it or not, math occurs in the classroom throughout the day, not just at "math time."

This chapter is designed to offer you multiple ideas for students to use math as a gateway for extracting meaning from real life each day. Opportunities for primary and intermediate students have been categorized but individual age, grade, or developmental levels have not. Simply modify or adjust each one as it best meets the developmental needs of your students.

You may be orchestrating many of the following opportunities already. If you discover at least one new possibility, then this book has been a success.

THE GOAL OF DAILY MATH OPPORTUNITIES

The primary goal of providing daily math opportunities is to build students' innate sense of number and their confidence in their ability to manipulate numbers at will and with ease. These are critical attributes for success in learning math at higher levels as well as during elementary school years. Leslie Hart calls these attributes a sense of "number-ness" and capacity for "flexing" numbers. The following is excerpted from his book, *"Anchor" Math: The Brain-Compatible Approach to Learning Math.*[1] The term "anchor math" refers to the importance of creating mental "anchors" for students through use of real life examples.

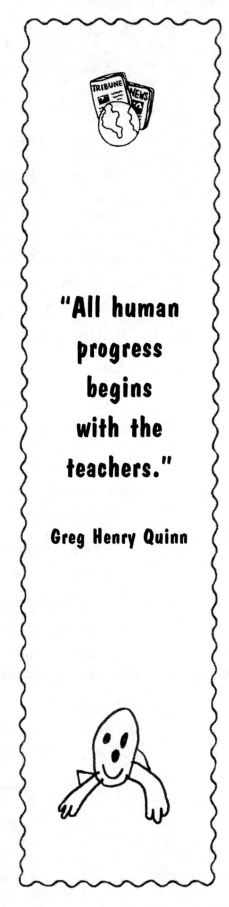

"All human progress begins with the teachers."

Greg Henry Quinn

"N-ness"

Let us assume that a particular student is able to

—Name the digit . . . "five"

—Write the digit

—Count off objects to match the digit

It still may be true that the student does not have the sense of that number, a sense that we can call "five-ness." *This sense of number* constitutes one of the main foundational elements of grasping math and being able to do or interpret math with ease and confidence. Some people like to say that the student "feels" the number—which is all right if you like that expression.

Another way to put it is to say that the student has acquired a sense of "shape" for that number and a direct approach, not a "counting" approach.

For instance, if the student hears "five" and then counts one-two-three-four-five, that is a slow and cumbersome way, as compared with directly feeling "five-ness."

This sense of "n-ness" can readily be encouraged and developed by the teacher . . . and, as we shall see, it can be applied not only to the digits but to many numbers as they are "anchored."

Suppose we ask a 10-year-old student: "What is the difference between numbers 23 and 24?" One student may reply, "24 is one more than 23." That is correct but not the reply we are seeking.

Another student says, "Oh, they are very different! 23 is a stiff, awkward number while 24 is wonderful—it can be the hours in a day, or two dozen, or 4 x 6, or 3 x 8. . . . I can do all sorts of things with it." We can exult, "Ah, this student has really learned the "anchor" math way; this student *feels* the number." Numbers have shapes and characters and personalities, much as do people. Math becomes much more interesting and easier to do when "the numbers come alive!"[1]

"Flexing"

We can use the problems of scanty three-ness to illustrate a simple technique for exploring numbers and patterns to which I'll attach the name "flexing." If you don't care for that term for this activity, use another or create your own. The idea is simple: *push the number, or pattern, or quantity around* in all the ways you can think of.

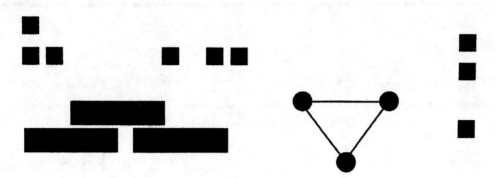

Flex . . . and find patterns.

Developing a sense of N-ness and a capacity for flexing are clearly essential building blocks to mathematic understanding and ability to apply math concepts and skills to real life situations and problems. Hart's discussion invites us to re-examine the content of our math lesson planning. The following levels of engagement are intended to jog your thinking about how to orchestrate student transition to strong competencies in mathematics.*

LEVELS OF ENGAGEMENT

Before selecting from the following practical applications for daily math opportunities in the classroom and school, assess your students. How well developed is their sense of number-ness? (Is their intuitive guess within the ball park of the exact answer) and how large are the numbers they have a good, concrete sense of (up to 10, up to a hundred, a thousand)? How well to they understand the math concept you are trying to teach them? How familiar are they with the context of the problem to be solved? If you think your students have a ways to go here, select activities accordingly. Level 1 suggestions offer the highest levels of engagement of the senses and require the least prior knowledge or experience in order to apply the mathematical concepts involved. Level 3 activities provide the least sensory input and require the highest levels of prior experience with math and the context of the problem to be solved.

(* Excerpted from *"Anchor" Math* by Leslie Hart.)

Assess the proposed activities against the three sliding scales below. Introduction of a concept should be followed by activities whose characteristics are described along the far left of all three continuums and progress through activities described along the far right of the continuums.

Rich sensory input
via all 19 senses

Sensory input limited
to 2 senses

$$5 \qquad 4 \qquad 3 \qquad 2 \qquad 1$$

Context of problem is
familiar and meaningful

Context is unfamiliar and/
or not meaningful

$$5 \qquad 4 \qquad 3 \qquad 2 \qquad 1$$

Numbers involved are within
child's range of sense of N-ness

Numbers are so large or so
small they are meaningless

$$5 \qquad 4 \qquad 3 \qquad 2 \qquad 1$$

Levels of Engagement: Level 1 Activities

Level 1 activities are to be used when students' level of understanding of the math concept or skill to be learned is tenuous or mistaken. The purpose of Level 1 activities is to provide the key ingredient for the human brain—meaningfulness. All involve mathematical applications to "here and now" occurrences—experienceable, firsthand, hands on. Examples of Level 1 Activities include the following:

Study trips. Almost any aspect of a study trip that has been experienced through the 19 senses makes an ideal context for math problems. The powerful ingredients of such a context, from the teacher's point of view, is that all of the students have a common experience from which to draw (the pitiless line between students with so-called advantaged and disadvantaged backgrounds disappears) and the range of possible problems to examine guarantees high interest by each and every student. See Chapter 10, Math Challenges in the Real World.

Micro-communities. Whether schoolwide, "house," or individual classroom, immersion into rich simulations of real life provides a steady flow of life-like opportunities to practice a wide range of mathematic concepts and skills. See Chapter 11: Practical Applications: Micro-Communities—Reality-Based Community Simulations.

Newspaper. A newspaper is a wealth of current knowledge and provides for real life mathematical exploration, problem-solving, and problem-producing opportunities. In fact, there are too many to list in this chapter. Please turn to the chapter "Theme math" for an additional menu of primary and intermediate possibilities.

Primary. By creating your own one- or two-page monthly class newspaper, students can have the opportunity to use the same mathematical concepts used to publish a daily city newspaper. In addition to reading and writing processes, students will have to measure, "paste up," figure costs, create surveys and distribute the newspaper, on a monthly basis.

Intermediate. By expanding the above example, intermediate students could publish the paper more often and increase its size. Also, you may want to include community events.

Class orders. Through the course of the school year, items to be ordered by class members pop up from time to time. Let the students handle the job. The most common on-going, task is, of course, ordering books. For those of you who offer Lucky, Troll, Scholastic, or other book orders for your students, think about allowing them to actually do the order themselves. Depending on the age and abilities of your students, each cooperative learning group can have real life application opportunities by counting and tallying orders, actually computing totals, counting money collected, figuring bonus points earned and how those points could be used to benefit the class. When the books arrive, students can count, sort, and match books with individual orders. If an error has been made by the book company, perhaps a student(s) could be responsible for writing a letter to the company explaining the problem. These examples could apply to primary or intermediate students.

Wellness. Integrating math skills into the everyday health and wellness of our bodies not only provides unlimited mathematical opportunities but teaches students how to take care of

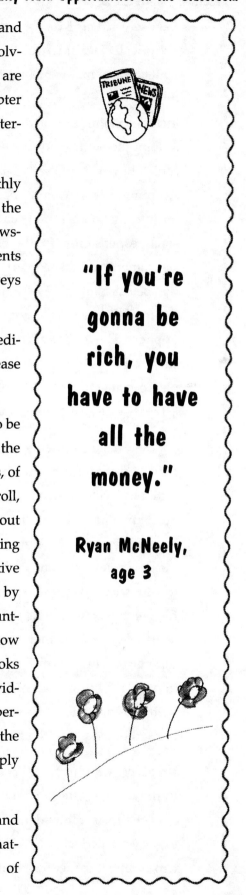

"If you're gonna be rich, you have to have all the money."

Ryan McNeely, age 3

themselves. Peg Kiser, a teacher in Indiana, has created a program know as "PHATS," "Physically Healthy And Technically Sound." This holistic wellness program teaches students how to make the best nutritional decisions and to design a fitness program just for themselves! For example, choices allowed students for cardiovascular fitness could include biking, use of the treadmill, Nordic Track, or stepper, and not just doing laps around the field. All of the physical fitness activities are noncompetitive, individual, and fun! "Physical fitness is based on motivation in movement experiences," reports Peg. Keeping track of weight, body mass index, and appropriate nutritional decisions based on information gleaned mathematically empower the individual students to take personal responsibility for themselves and to look at the consequences of their choices. These assessments are taken every twelve weeks. While participating in this program, students will be calculating: How much? How many servings? What are the percentages of fat in the foods I'm eating? What are the total calories? How much did I grow? What is my upper and lower body strength? Has it increased? What is my body mass index and other such inquiries? If you would like more information about this comprehensive program, please contact: PHATS, c/o Peg Kiser, 336 E. Washington, Winchester, Indiana 47394, (317) 584-8561, or e-mail: Kiserian@aol.com.

By teaching students how to take their own pulse before, during, and after daily exercise, they can become aware of their own heart rates at different levels of activity. During different levels of activity, students can estimate what they anticipate their heart rates to be. Estimations can be charted, then compared to their actual counts. Each cooperative learning group can calculate their group's range, mode, median, and mean heart rates for the day, week, or month. Group statistics can be compared and hypotheses generated as to why some groups may have greater averages than others. Diane Silveira, of John Reed Elementary School in Rohnert Park, California, has her students keep track of their daily heartbeat by taking their pulse at rest and after their daily exercise and then figuring the difference. This information is recorded in each student's math journal in a special section on a "Thump-Thump" page (see example on the next page). Students then display their findings after a given amount of time by creating bar graphs based upon the data they collected about their own body.

Graphing. Children of all ages are gatherers of information. Their curiosity usually comes in the form of questions: where? who? why? how? when? how many? and how much? And their natural tendency is to want to share what they are excited about. Graphing is eagerly learned as a way to tell others about things they saw and learned on their study trip or about something that actually happened in class. "Graphing provides a way for

Thump Thump

	At Rest	Movement	Difference
Sept 7	19 x 4 ――― 72	25 x 4 ――― 110	110 − 72 ――― 38
Sept 15	21 x 4 ――― 84	21 x 4 ――― 84 I didn't move a lot.	84 − 84 ――― 00
Sept 25	15 x 4 ――― 60	22 x 4 ――― 88	88 − 60 ――― 28
Oct 4	16 x 4 ――― 64	23 x 4 ――― 92	92 − 64 ――― 32
Oct 18 Jump rope	22 x 4 ――― 88	39 x 4 ――― 156	156 − 88 ――― 68
Nov 6 Soccer	17 x 4 ――― 68	31 x 4 ――― 124	124 − 68 ――― 56

children to organize information clearly so that they can grasp its meaning more readily."[2] Additionally, graphing allows them to see quantities in proportion to each other and/or a fixed quantity and presents an opportunity for students to construct their own knowledge in a way that makes sense to them. The content can be personal and thus playful or professional and thus more formal.

Graphing can be a Level I input activity if the content that is to be graphed is the result of multi-sensory input from "being there" experiences.

Children should learn how to use a variety of graphs based on which would enhance the analytic process and which would best communicate the data to another person. For starters, students should become adept users of the following: bar graphs, circle graphs, axis graphs, Venn circles, the simple column chart, and mindmaps.

- **Bar** and **circle** graphs assist the observer to compare quantities of numerous items.

- **Axis** graphs assist in observing directions or trends or how much of which of two ingredients must be increased or decreased in order to reach a desired goal.

- **Venn circles** assist the observer in comparing two entities for differences and similarities.

- **Simple column chart**s separate out the data by designated characteristics (e.g., bookkeeping formats and decision-making formats such as "P.M.I." for examining the plus, minus, and interesting effects of various options during decision-making).

- **Mindmaps** are capable of presenting a large amount of data and, most importantly, showing the interrelationships among pieces of data. Because it is a visual format, it gives the brain more clues for analyzing relationships and remembering the big idea and its relevant details.

Graphing for Level One activities should always be based upon information directly experienced by the students and, to the extent possible, should provide visuals to remind students what the "it" is that the graphs quantify and illustrate. For examples, see the ABC graphs in appendix A.

Graphing provides a window for teacher observation, an authentic way to assess what students know and how they can manipulate data to make sense of the situation at hand. It provides a way of focusing on standard number 11 of the NCTM Standards, the importance of collecting, organizing, and describing data.

Estimating. Estimations can be about anything: time, weight, age, cost, quantity, etc. The important thing to remember about Level I activities is that the estimating should be about things that provide full sensory input at the moment of math study. Also, remember that estimating is different from guesstimating. A guess is a guess because you have no reference points; a mathematical estimate is based on prior experience with the item, a knowledge of simple math formulas (such as those for volume, area, pints to a gallon, etc.), and a sense of N-ness. Guessing does not enhance math education; estimating does.

Incorporating an estimation of the week is a fun and easy way to strengthen estimation skills. Using theme-related items in a jar, in a bag, or in a cup, students can estimate and then calculate the weight, length, width, or height of objects. Recording should utilize narrative and various kinds of graphs.

Add a twist to this activity by giving students the answer! For example, if you have three cups filled with varying amounts of seeds, tell them that one of the cups has a specific number/weight in it. By estimating the volume of the known quantity and comparing it to the other two cups, the students can then estimate the quantities in the other cups. Weekly estimations are kept in their math journals.

At the next parent gathering in your classroom, set up several estimations for your students and their parents to take part in. (You will want to do this after the students have had adequate time to develop this skill as estimation skills improve with experience.) I have done this several times, and most of the time, the estimates from the students are closer to the actual number than those estimates of the parents! Parents are impressed!

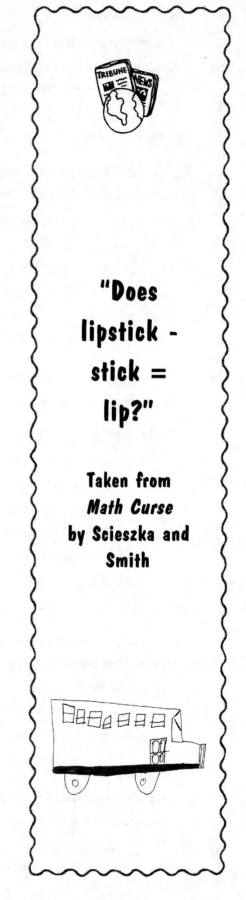

"Does lipstick - stick = lip?"

Taken from *Math Curse* by Scieszka and Smith

Remember: estimating does not mean simply guessing. Estimating means you have some mathematical information to begin with, e.g, volume of a jar and approximate volume of a jelly bean. Guessing without premise or hypothesis is antithetical to teaching math as problem-solving tools and processes.

Levels of Engagement: Level 2 Activities

The events, situations, things, places used for applying mathematical concepts may not be within students' range of experiences. Therefore, the teacher must create an immersion environment in which the context for the math problems is replicated in the classroom in ways that evoke as many senses as possible. Immersion settings are the bridge between concrete, real world experiences for learning math and abstract thinking about math in which students apply math concepts to situations never seen before. In this level the teacher dances between asking students to apply well known math concepts to unknown situations and unfamiliar math concepts applied to familiar situations.

The following suggestions are in addition to the activities identified in Level 1, each of which could be used as a format for Level 2 activities with appropriate increases in difficulty.

Daily Oral Math. Daily Oral Math, D.O.M., is a great to begin each day or the beginning of daily work on your theme. The purpose of D.O.M is to introduce and/or reinforce selected computational skills. The context for these skills should always be from the content of the week's thematic work, e.g. distance between two cities being studied, cost of items in historical perspective, speed, etc. When all students have completed their work, a student, group of students, or the teacher may solve the problem, modeling correct form and computation. Daily Oral Math problems may be recorded in each student's math journal for on-going skill records.

Primary. A review of the computation of the basic operations, as well as a real life application problem based on your current curriculum could become a D.O.M. problem. For example, if you are learning about insects, students could calculate how many legs on two insects, three insects, or ten insects. Students could act out, draw, or symbolically represent how they formulated their answer.

Intermediate. You can challenge intermediate students by expanding on the ideas listed above. In addition, you can include skills such as a review of the formulas for computing area or distance of a location being studied.

Literature. Using literature can be a powerful way to integrate your curriculum and expand your math program at the same time. "Mathematics is a communication tool that works directly with the skill of reading and allows the student to use and understand data found in all school subjects and to interpret the logic and pattern found in those subjects. Reading and mathematics skills must go hand in hand for the student to become a successful learner."[3] When selecting a piece of literature to integrate into your theme, it is important not to be narrow in your thinking. It is not necessary to limit yourself to integrating literature solely on your social studies or science content. Think bigger. Integration can occur by aligning math concepts with major concepts from other disciplines, Lifelong Guidelines, or LIFESKILLS (See appendix B.) To assist you in integrating mathematics and literature, I would like to recommend the book, *Math Through Children's Literature* by Kathryn L. Braddon, Nancy J. Hall, and Dale Taylor, available through Books For Educators. This book uses the NCTM Standards to organize major concepts for the elementary level and is divided into K-3 and 4-6 categories. Numerous children's literature books with accompanying activities have been selected for each category. These introduce or reinforce specific mathematical concepts in accordance with each standard.

There are barrelfuls of wonderful resources for connecting math with other subject areas. Ask any children's librarian or bookstore.*

Graphing. As mentioned in Level 1, sources of information and problems to be solved are everywhere—reading a daily newspaper, listening to a news report, connecting with one of the many information superhighways of a computer networking system. Information bombards us from all directions, providing multiple daily opportunities to organize, analyze, and communicate this information mathematically,

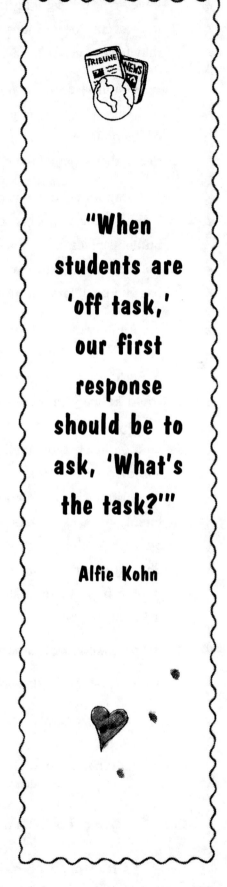

"When students are 'off task,' our first response should be to ask, 'What's the task?'"

Alfie Kohn

---

* Many bookstores specialize in subject area integration. For example, J&J's Bookworm in Thousand Oaks, California, provides its customers a list of math related literature books on request. Call 805/492-4152 or e-mail: bookjjworm@aol.com

developing critical skills for students. Content for Level 2 graphing should come from subjects, events, or locations that students have been studying at some depth and for which they have a feel of N-ness.

Graphs are such a valuable tool for analysis and reporting that it should be applied to a variety of situations and done frequently, even daily. Students enjoyed our "graph-of-the-day" which was usually theme-related. If the content is meaningful to the students, they enjoyed the challenge.

Graph-for-the-day is easy to structure; simply put a question in a pocket chart or on a piece of chart paper, a white board, an overhead, or even in the students' math journals. Students place their name card next to their choice of task and then respond to the question or task in the form of a graph. Intermediate students can construct their own graphs, based on the data and using their knowledge of different kinds of graphs.

Another of my students' favorite topics for graphing was author/illustrator studies. Not only is it a great way to integrate subjects into your theme, it gives students an opportunity to critique a book—to give their opinion about it, what they like and how it could be made more interesting, etc. For example, if you're studying about frogs and toads you may choose to read *Frog and Toad Together* by Arnold Lobel as a read-aloud to your entire class or small group literature study. Once you have the opportunity to read and discuss this book, read other books by the same author, comparing and contrasting the writing and illustration styles. Venn diagrams can then be used to compare the different books, characters, or settings. Graphs could then be constructed showing which books from the author study represented the students' favorites (see examples below). Student-generated story problems based on this data would then be conceptualized and written by individual students for the class to solve. With primary students, consider using picture books.

Examples of story problems developed from author study graph:

- How many students took part and voted on their favorite book by Arnold Lobel?

- Which book was our class favorite? least favorite?

- What is the total number of books that were our class favorites that were about a frog and a toad?

- Which book did not represent a favorite of anyone in the class?

- How many of the books by Arnold Lobel that are included in our graph have an animal as as main character?

- Did another class do a class study on Arnold Lobel? If so, how do their favorites compare to ours?

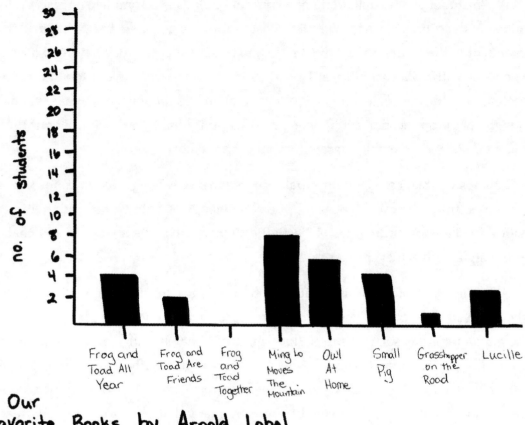

Our
Favorite Books by Arnold Lobel

Levels of Engagement: Level 3 Activities

Level 3 math requires a firm foundation from Level 1 and 2 activities. Students' grasp of mathematical concepts must be considerably deeper than that required of Level 1 and 2 activities and students must be more adept at learning through verbally described situations rather than those they directly experience. This is the level at which students use math to help make sense of things that they have not yet experienced or don't yet understand—things so huge or so miniscule that only math can begin to help them understand the implications, e.g., 4 parts per million as a lethal dose of poison translated into conditions along the local river: How many gallons of that toxin can be poured into the river before a health hazard level is reached? What about low flow times during the summer? Etc.

Level 3 activities use math as a tool to more fully understand issues within other subject areas. Math is experienced by students as a tool for real life.

COMMON PITFALLS

When students' understanding of a concept or skills is incomplete or inaccurate, the context of the concept provides limited sensory input (e.g., paper and pencil drill) and is unfamiliar to the students (e.g., the problem to be solved is one they have had little or no experience with), plan activities at Level 1. Avoid moving into Level 2 too quickly. Make sure you provide adequate time to develop a real understanding of the what, when, how, and why of the application and to then practice application to various situations until the student develops a mental program for longterm memory.

Perhaps the biggest planning pitfall occurs when we design activities for the entire class based upon the capabilities and prior knowledge of a student(s) with high mathematical intelligence. Even at Level 1 activities, where are endless ways to add challenge for the high math achiever.

Another source of pitfalls is tradition, activities long considered "good" strategies but when viewed through the lens of recent brain research can no longer be recommended. There are numerous such examples that are, unfortunately, quite common in our classrooms. I highly recommend you use the brain research described in Chapter 4 together with the discussion of Levels of Engagement to reexamine your old trusty, seemingly tried and true activities. I discovered there were many that I had to precede with activities from Levels 1 and 2. A few I even had to leave behind altogether.

INSTRUCTIONAL STRUCTURES

Many instructional structures are inherent in the content of the math to be performed and thus vary from day to day. However, three structures I found to be invaluable on a daily basis were mental math, writing word problems, and math journals.

Mental Math. Many teachers shy away from mental math problems for students, believing that they are too hard for many students, especially those having difficulty with math in general. Thus, little time is devoted to mental arithmetic yet "much of the math you need as an adult involves only mental arithmetic."[3] Mental math is a powerful tool and we owe it to all our students, to provide them the necessary practice to develop proficiency in mental math for adulthood since so much of how we use math in our lives is in our heads. However, do keep in mind that the content for early experiences with mental math should be based on real world things or events that students have experienced directly and within the past couple of days or, better yet, about something happening right now.

Many years ago, I came across the mental math game "I HAVE, WHO HAS" shown on the next two pages. Each question is listed on a separate index card. Cards are randomly distributed to each student and numbered. The student holding card #1 begins by reading the problem on his/her card (Do not number the other cards.). Other students have to compute in their heads as each card is read to see if the answer is written on their card. After giving the correct answer written on his/her card, that student then reads the problem on his/her card and the process continues until the last card has been read and an answer given. See an example of the game on the next page.

I have used the examples that follow with students as young as second grade. Create your own based on the ability level of your students and the content being studied, e.g., measurement, estimation, telling time, etc. Students enjoy creating their own sets of I HAVE, WHO HAS, working individually or in partners.

Primary grade examples include asking students to figure out "in their heads" such things as how old are you (in years and months?) If you have a brother or sister, how many years older or younger are you than your sibling? How old will you be in 4 years? 8 years? 10 years? etc. How old will your brother or sister be in 4 years, 8 years? 10 years? etc. How much money will you need to buy specific items? Playing the game, "I'm thinking of a number," is another great example of mental math. For example, "I'm thinking of a number that is greater than 20, is less than 30 and has a 5 in the ones place (25)." Allow students the opportunity to think of the number and give clues to the other students.

Expanding on the game, "I'm thinking of a number," you can provide intermediate students with challenging mental math problems. For example, "The number I'm thinking of has three digits, the number in the tens place is a five, and the sum of the remaining two numbers is twelve." The answer could be 755 or 557. You can vary the level of difficulty depending on ages of your students. These mental activities sharpen mental calculations. This game lends itself nicely to transition times in the classroom.

I Have / Who Has?

Author Unknown

1. I have 7.   Who has 3 less?
2. I have 4.   Who has twice as many?
3. I have 8.   Who has 4 more?
4. I have 12.   Who has 1/2 of this?
5. I have 6.   Who has 5 divided by 5?
6. I have 1.   Who has this multiplied by 9?
7. I have 9.   Who has this plus 3 divided by 4?
8. I have 3.   Who has this doubled plus 4?
9. I have 10.   Who has a dozen more?
10. I have 22.   Who has this divided by 11?
11. I have 2.   Who has this minus 2 times 6?
12. I have 0.   Who has 19 more?
13. I have 19.   Who has this plus 1 times 2?
14. I have 40.   Who has this less 10?
15. I have 30.   Who has this divided by 6?
16. I have 5.   Who has this plus 1 times 3?
17. I have 18.   Who has this and two more?
18. I have 20.   Who has double this plus 1 more?
19. I have 41.   Who has 2 less?
20. I have 39.   Who has 5 less?
21. I have 34.   Who has 1 more?
22. I have 35.   Who has this minus 2?
23. I have 33.   Who has double this?
24. I have 66.   Who has this divided by 11 plus 5?
25. I have 11.   Who has 6 more?
26. I have 17.   Who has 3 less?
27. I have 14.   Who has 1/2 of this multiplied by 3?
28. I have 21.   Who has this and 10 more?
29. I have 31   Who has this plus 4, divided by 5?

[Add additional plays to the game based on your students'
levels of readiness to succeed and have fun.]

Start   #1
"I have 7.
Who has 3
less?"

"I have 4.
Who has twice
as many?"

"I have 8.
Who has 4
more?"

"Telling Time"
I Have / Who Has?
Author Unknown

1. I have 10:00. Who has 1 hour earlier?

2. I have 9:00.   Who has thirty minutes later?

3. I have 9:30.   Who has one hour earlier?

4. I have 8:30.   Who has five minutes later?

5. I have 8:35.   Who has ten minutes earlier?

6. I have 8:25.   Who has one hour earlier?

7. I have 7:25   Who has ten minutes earlier?

8. I have 7:15.   Who has fifteen minutes later?

9. I have 7:30.   Who has thirty minutes earlier?

10. I have 7:00. Who has one hour later?

11. I have 8:00. Who has two hours earlier?

12. I have 6:00. Who has half an hour later?

13. I have 6:30. Who has two hours earlier?

14. I have 4:30. Who has fifteen minutes later?

15. I have 4:45. Who has an hour earlier?

16. I have 3:45. Who has half an hour earlier?

17. I have 3:15. Who has fifteen minutes later?

18. I have 3:30. Who has two hours earlier?

19. I have 1:30. Who has half an hour earlier?

20. I have 1:00. Who has an hour later?

21. I have 2:00. Who has two hours earlier?

22. I have 12:00. Who has half an hour later?

23. I have 12:30. Who has half an hour and fifteen minutes later?

24. I have 1:15. Who has one hour later?

25. I have 2:15. Who has two hours earlier?

26. I have 12:15. Who has two hours earlier?

27. I have 10:15. Who has forty-five minutes earlier?

28. I have 9:30.

[Add additional plays to the game based on your students' levels of readiness to succeed and have fun.]

| Start   #1 |
| "I have 10:00. Who has one hour earlier?" |

| "I have 9:00. Who has 30 minutes later?" |

| "I have 9:30. Who has one hour earlier?" |

Writing Story Problems

Having children write their own story problems about a given topic of study is a great way to integrate math into your curriculum. After a great deal of modeling about how to write a story problem so that the questions you are asking is clear in the reader's mind, ask your students to write at least three story problems based on your content. Then, choose one from each set of the three stories for the class to work on. Be sure you write the author's name next to the problem he or she has written. Do not correct or clarify the problems. It is up to each student to correct the problem he or she has written for the rest of the class. Students learn very quickly what happens if a problem is not written in a clear manner after ten classmates come to the author's desk asking him or her to explain what is meant. Allowing children the opportunities to be problem creators, will support and enhance their abilities to be better problem solvers.

As you can see by the examples below, story problems written by students can be written at all levels of ability and with much more creativity and relevance than story problems found in a textbook. Also, reading something written by a friend is always engaging. The following examples were written by second and third graders as part of a theme-related study about frogs and toads.

Student-developed word problems

Examples from primary grades:

- There were two frogs on a log. They were joined by three toads passing by. Then one toad ran away. One frog married the other frog and they had two baby tadpoles. How many frogs and toads were there? (Written by Emily)

- There were fifteen frogs and nine toads. Add them all together and see what you get. (Written by Allison)

- There were three frogs, Tommy, Tadly, and Toadly. Tommy had six cookies. How many would each one get to have the same amount of cookies? You have to pretend that frogs eat cookies. (Written by Keara)

- There are six frogs in each pond. There are twenty-four ponds in the swamp. How many frogs are in the whole swamp? (Written by Steve)

Examples from intermediate grades:

- A Mascarene frog holds the world's distance record for jumping. In a single jump, one of them jumped 17.5 ft.! What would the equivalent distance be if we measured it in metrics? (Written by Matt)

- The change from a newly hatched tadpole to a fully formed froglet takes about 12 to 16 weeks; the time is greatly affected by water temperature and food supply. How many days does this time range represent? (Written by Natalie)

- The Chilean red-spotted toad has adapted to living at high altitudes and has been found as high as 13,000 ft. in the Andes Mountains. What is the highest mountain range nearest to where you live? Could the Chilean red-spotted toad live there? Why or why not? (Written by Shawn) (You may need to do some research to learn more about the elevations in your area.)

Math Journals. Math journals provide an ongoing tool to give feedback/assessment to you, the teacher, the student, and the parents about the student's understanding and application abilities of mathematical concepts. The reasons why math journals should be incorporated on a daily basis and how to incorporate them are multifaceted. Please see Chapter 5, "Language and Math," for a menu of primary and intermediate implementation opportunities.

In this chapter I have highlighted numerous ways to incorporate the application of mathematical concepts and basic skills into the daily routine of your classroom. By doing so, the desired result of what your students can do is to see the math connections in their everyday lives and to understand that, "Skills are to mathematics what scales are to music or spelling is to writing. The objective of learning is to write, to play music, or to solve problems-not just to master skills.[4]

For Further Study

Anchor Math
by Leslie A. Hart

Storytime, Mathtime: Discovering Math in Children's Literature (for grades 1-3)
by Patricia Satariano

Math Through Children's Literature
by Braddon, Hall, and Taylor

Chapter 13
Practical Applications:
Math at Home—
A Guide to Assist Parents

Creating a mathematical environment at home for your child is a wonderful way to enhance your child's number sense and math confidence. But how do you create such an environment? The good news is, you already have. It is a natural by-product of living our lives in the late 20th century. Grocery lists, games played, furniture you may have in your house, telling time, and observing nature all provide these natural opportunities. This chapter is designed to support you in helping your child see that math is everywhere.

"There's no place like home... there's no place like home."

Dorothy

MATH OPPORTUNITIES IN AND AROUND THE HOME

Where are all of these math opportunities at home? Where should you look for "the math?" Let's take an imaginary tour through a home to find out. Let's begin in the kitchen as it seems to be at the center of our day-to-day living.

Kitchen

The kitchen is the most used room in the American house. Fortunately, it is also the richest in math opportunities.

Grocery shopping. Sleuthing out the best buy or coupon clipping, saving swapping, and redemption are great projects for children. Couponing even has all the characteristics of a lifelong hobby that can grow to the level of self-employment. Let

your children keep 30% of what they redeem as salary for their effort and make sure that you alert them to the fact that many stores often double or even triple the value listed on the coupon. Practice in addition, subtraction, multiplication (especially figuring percentages), and division is guaranteed.

Budgeting. Creating and sticking to a budget by prioritizing needs before wants is an invaluable ways to explore our inner core values as well as to become familiar with the real-world costs of items around us. Both are great preparation for life as an adult.

Don't overlook the time-honored weekly allowance, however big or small, and especially the opportunity to earn extra for completing additional tasks in order to buy a treasured item such as a baseball glove, a computer program, or a ticket to a favorite event. Have children graph their progress toward that highly anticipated purchase.

For older children, encourage them to use various decision-making frameworks such as the simple but useful three column headings (+, -, N) to graphically illustrate the positive, negative, and neutral consequences of a pending decision.

Cooking. Cooking is rich in skill practice—measurements (both standard and metric) in recipes, time frames for cooking or baking, temperature, and time adjustments for quantities, etc. "For boys and girls alike, cooking and baking offer a splendid group of activities cutting across subject boundaries. Recipes for cupcakes, a birthday cake, snacks, or whatever can be worked out for quantity, printed out on wall charts, then followed (a reading activity demanding accuracy), as well as being a measuring process with obvious real purpose. Temperature and time must be controlled and the size of pots or pans checked. The whole function is drenched in arithmetic, especially if the overall project involves costing, buying supplies and, at times, packaging, weighing, and pricing for sale."[1]

With a bit of nudging, the kitchen can be viewed as the ultimate chemical factory that it is. So don't overlook the science opportunities here as well as the math experiences. (See *Kitchen Chemistry: Science Experiments You Can Do at Home* by Robert Gardner; available through Books for Educators, 253/630-6908.)

Cereal. Most kids love to read cereal boxes while they're eating their morning cereal. Cereal boxes are filled with math concepts! How many servings per box? Is the serving size on the box the amount that you eat per serving? Is it more or less than the average serving? What is the average cost per serving? Which ingredient is predominate? (It will be the first one listed; ingredients by law are always listed by percent of content, greatest to least.) Is there a recipe on the box? Which ingredients do you need? Try doubling the recipe.

Refrigerator door. Use double sets of magnetic numbers and letters so that you and your child can write messages to each other on the refrigerator door. Include number concepts such as times and dates in your messages.

Clocks. Most kitchens have a clock, ideal for reinforcing the concept of telling time. I encourage you to use analog clocks because of the opportunities to deal with fractions—quarter to, half an hour, etc.

Many children are capable of reading a digital clock but do not possess a concept of time. If you are using a digital clock, ask your young child which number will change the quickest, the number on the right or the left? See if he or she can predict which number will come up next.

Calendar. Many families keep a calendar of family events up somewhere in the kitchen. Use this calendar to compute how many days, weeks, or months until a certain event. Your child might like to create his or her own calendar illustrating his or her activities for the week.

Recycling. Recycling cans, newspapers, and glass are ways to help our planet, generate added income, and use many mathematical concepts and skills at the same time. By recycling cans and/or newspapers, children can estimate and then calculate how many pounds they can save and how much money will be collected. A graph or chart could be kept to keep track of the information. Again, you might want to assist the child to turn this into a moneymaking venture, 25 percent for the child and 75 percent to the family grocery kitty or to the family's gifts to charity. (Be sure to involve your child in the selecting of the charities to receive the family's donations.)

Growth chart. On a door or wall, keep a measurement growth chart of your child or children. Record growth periodically. Ask your child(ren) to predict how much they

"Alone we can do so little; together we can do so much."

Helen Keller

"Children may close their ears to advice but open their eyes to example."

Anonymous

think they have grown from the previous time they were measured. Compare actual measurement with predictions. Use measurement terminology to explain the outcomes to your children. "John is taller than you are by two inches. That is one inch taller than he was the last time we measured."

Laundry Room

Measuring soap for laundry or other cleaning purposes provides a real "need to know." Older children can cost out per load (water, electricity or gas, detergent, and even replacement cost of clothing.) Young children can count how many socks are in the laundry basket and figure out how many pairs there are (or should be!).

Dining Room

When setting the table, compute how many placemats, napkins, forks, knives, spoons, etc., you will need to set the table. How many items all together? How many trips to get the items carried to the table? Etc., etc.

Perhaps the dining room table is a place where you may wrap gifts or cut fabric to make clothes. Ask your child to help you estimate and measure how much gift wrap, ribbon, or fabric you will need for your project.

Living/Family Room

This may be a place where family members play games, enjoy playing cards, or carry out their hobbies and responsibilities for operating the household. The following list of games and card games will provide multiple opportunities to engage your child in math skills without him or her even knowing it.

Board games to encourage development of a strong "number sense"

Monopoly	Checkers
Stratego	Yahtzee
Sorry (board game)	LIFE (board game)
Dominoes	Battleship
Triominoes	
Scrabble (scoring)	
Bowling (scoring)	
Bingo (for number recognition)	
Jigsaw puzzles (spatial relationships)	
Connect Four: The Vertical Checkers Game	

Card games to encourage development of a strong "number sense"

Salute	Go Fish
War	Crazy 8s
Concentration	Canasta
Pinochle	

You have to play these games on something. . . a table, perhaps. So, now let's look at the furniture. What are the angles, shapes, and design that allow your furniture to do what it is designed to do? Do you see symmetry in any of the furniture? In a design on a rug on the floor? In pottery?

Bedroom

Do you have a quilt on one or more beds in your home? What kinds of geometric shapes, angles, and colors create your quilt? Do you find these same shapes, angles, and colors in other places?

Does your child collect certain items such as toy cars, rocks, shells, stickers, etc.? Allow space and materials to help your child sort and classify these items. Eggshell cartons or tackle boxes are easy ways to store your child's collections once they have been sorted and classified.

Bathroom

The bathroom is a wealth of resources for applying math concepts and helping our planet at the same time! According to *50 Simple Things Kids Can Do to Save the Earth*, we are wasting too much water! Did you know that:

- When you shower, you use five gallons of water every minute. How much is that? Enough to fill 40 big glasses!

- A whole shower usually takes at least five minutes. So, every day you could use 25 gallons of water taking one shower. In a year, that's almost 10,000 gallons for your showers.

- Taking a bath uses even more water than showers—about twice as much.

- We use more water in our toilets than in any other place in our homes.

- Believe it or not, the water we flush down our toilets starts out as fresh drinking water!

- Each time you flush, your toilet uses about five to seven gallons of water!

- You can save up to 20,000 gallons of water a year by not letting the water run from your faucet.

- If you leave the water running while you brush your teeth, you can waste five gallons of water. How many cans of soda could you fill with five gallons?

- If you leave the water running while you wash the dishes, you can waste 30 gallons of water, enough to wash a whole car!

I highly recommend *50 Simple Things Kids Can Do to Save the Earth* to you and your family. It not only provides fascinating and useful math statistics galore but also offers solutions to the problems at hand. Published by Scholastic it may be purchased at most bookstores and is also available by mail through Books for Educators.

Home Maintenance

Home maintenance is the bedevilment of every home owner. A little preparation for the role would help make us better investors, initially and in the long run.

Responsibilities. The leaks in your finances are everywhere. Solutions include keeping track of the heating thermostat and water meter in relation to your monthly utility bills, analyzing your yard with an eye on water conservation, surveying your plumbing for leaks, and so forth. How much water will be saved with a low-flow shower head or by fixing a leaky faucet?

Enhancing decor. Take a look at the pictures and artwork in your home. Did the artist use lines, angles, or shapes to create the image? What kind of architecture is your house? What shapes do you see? What shapes make up other shapes? Does the design incorporate a particular style representing a time period or geographic area? What role does geometry play in creating this look?

By making rulers and tape measures available, you can encourage your child to engage in measurement activities as they naturally occur in your home. Opportunities for measuring are everywhere. Hanging or framing a picture, buying a piece of furniture (will it fit the intended space?), and recarpeting an area are all ways to incorporate measurement with your child.

Planning replacements and renovations. Whether we can bear to think about it or not, good long-term maintenance hinges on the art of planning when various items need replacing or resurfacing. Items such as carpet, linoleum, tile, walls, etc. need to be placed on a timeline and a budget created to ensure the money will be available when the action date arrives. Lots of math opportunities here! How much carpet at how much a square foot, with pad, with installation? Comparative shopping through the newspapers, radio, TV, and various advertising circulars. . . best quality for best price. The math and decision making are all but endless.

Are you planning to do any renovations to your home? Build a new patio cover? Deck? Enclose a garage? How should you figure out what you need? Figuring out dimensions, cost of building materials, and time are all events that require the application of mathematical skills. Include your child in such analyses and decisions. Even a very young child can help you figure out which is longer, shorter, heavier, lighter.

"It is better to build children than to repair adults."

Anon

"America's future walks through the doors of our schools each day."

Mary Jean LeTendre

Backyard

The backyard is a gold mine for math. Look below the ground and in the air as well as for earthbound things.

Weather. Keep a thermometer in your yard. Give your child practice understanding this concept by predicting (based on the temperature of the day before) and reading the temperatures. Ask your child, "Do you think the temperature will be warmer or cooler today?" Compare with predictions by radio, TV, and newspaper; what percentage of the time are they accurate? Variables to discuss could include the weather forecast (are storms expected?), expectations for weather given the calendar month, and whether certain plants need special care to endure specific temperatures.

Nature. Look for symmetry and geometry in nature such as shells, leaves, tree rings, growth rings on turtle shells, scales on fish (if you happen to have a body of water nearby or a goldfish on the dresser). Do you have a swimming pool in your backyard? Testing chemical levels of the water and maintaining a chemical balance of the water are all mathematical tasks. How about installing a rain gauge in your yard? Lots of fractions here!

Do you have a small corner of ground that can be given over to ongoing exploration? Provide some tools. Count every animal you encounter in the digging of a 1' x 1' x 1' hole. How about a five-minute snoop of a 1" x 1" square of lawn? Categorize the animals by number of legs, eyes or not, antennae or not and so forth. Then, how many of each piece of anatomy in all?

Sandbox. Playing with water and sand are excellent ways for children to learn about volume and capacity. Just provide your child with a selection of suitable containers, scoops for water and sand, and let your child experiment.

Communicating with Family and Friends

Buying stamps and figuring postage for household mail is another natural way in which mathematics are used throughout the house. Buy a mail scale. Ask your child to predict how much a specific piece of mail might weigh and what its cost would be. Compare your child's prediction with the actual cost.

Analyze your phone bill. If each long distance call were shortened by 10 percent, how much money would have been saved? Recalculate the taxes.

Chores

In addition to the static weekly allowance, set up additional tasks, at home and around the neighborhood, in ways that give children experience with real-world payment formulas, for example, payment per unit for picking up pine cones, slugs, or maple seed wings, per job for weeding this section of the yard, in addition to the common wage per hour. For per unit situations, e.g., a nickel per each edible fruit picked, have your child figure out how much he or she should be paid. Encourage your neighbors to structure their payment plans on a per item or per small job-within-a-job basis as well.

COMMUNITY-BASED ACTIVITIES

Community-based sources of math in action are infinite. Here are just a few to get you started on your own explorations.

Family outings/interests/events. High interest, high engagement activities are especially good for cementing math applications into long term memory.

Vacations. Vacations provide endless statistics to noodle and nudge numbers about: budgets, cost of hotels, food, gas, possible entrance fees for destination points; mapping out routes, computing trip miles, number of hours; and surveying family members to determine the most and least favorite sights, etc.

In the car. Keep track of road signs and shapes, counting how many signs that you see that are octagons, circles, triangles, etc.

Restaurants. When going out for dinner, "menu math" is a fun and interesting way to incorporate math. Tell your children what your budget is for a meal at a particular restaurant. Let them help decide if your family can afford to have appetizers, dessert, or something to drink other than water. Could you have a less expensive main course to allow for these other courses? Are there less expensive meals of the same kind at other restaurants? Would you get the most for your money if two people split a meal but ordered an extra salad? What percentage of the total meal should you leave for a tip? Has this been accounted for in your budget? You may want to bring a calculator to dinner!

Architecture around town. When out and about, pay close attention to buildings that you see. Angles, triangles, cubes, pyramids, squares, parallelograms, and circles are all concepts used to create buildings and their surroundings. For example, go on a "triangle hunt" (or any other shape) while on a family outing. With older children, talk about what would happen if a different shape had been used in the construction and make the models at home with toothpicks or straws, etc. This is geometry in action!

Newspapers. Subscription rates, cost of advertising, and reading graphs and charts that appear in the paper, the sports section, and information in the classified ads to be bought and sold all provide a springboard to exploration of math relevancy.

Playground. When playing on the equipment, i.e.; monkey bars, slide, seesaw, etc., children are "doing math and physics with their whole bodies. They will learn to verbalize their experiences as they hear you using terms such as up, down, around, high, higher, low, lower, under, over, across, beginning, end, fast, slow, big, little, horizontal, vertical, and parallel."[2]

Sports. Keeping track of games won and lost, scores, and individual player statistics are opportunities for manipulating lots of numbers. Be sure to use aspects that are of great interest to each child.

Parties. Planning for a party is a mathematical extravaganza for any child! How many guests? How many invitations? How many stamps will we need? How much will they cost? How much food? Decorations? Will there be party favors? If so, how many? What will the cost be? If we are able to purchase some of the items on sale, how much money can we save?

Don't forget to interview other family members or neighbors about how they use math skills in their lives.

INVESTING FOR KIDS

Childhood and becoming an investor traditionally have not come hand in hand. But, thanks to investments designed just for kids, we will begin to see this more and more. Children can save their allowance or baby-sitting money to invest in stocks, bonds, mutual funds and more. Some parents have agreed to match funds invested or seed the account with $100 to begin. "The payoffs can be enormous. At a minimum, children will see their math skills improve and knowledge of the economy expand. At best, they will retire wealthy. Barry Murphy, Marketing Director for the National Association of Investors Corporation, recently stated that, "If you could start all the kids in this country as investors at age 5 or 6, they all would be millionaires in their 50s, and they wouldn't have to worry about Social Security not being there." For additional information on investments designed just for kids, you may want to contact:

Stein Roe Young Investor Fund
800/338-2250

Twentieth Century Giftrust
800/345-2021

National Association of Investors Corp.
810/583-6242

The Moneypaper Guide to
Dividend Reinvestment Plans
800/388-9993

KIDS AS ENTREPRENEURS

It's hard to get a job when you're only ten years old but many children possess an entrepreneurial spirit! Making greeting cards or wrapping paper, creating jewelry from telephone wire, selling lemonade, collecting recyclable items, and doing chores for others are a few of the creative ways some kids have gone "into business" for themselves. For more information about how to help kids become entrepreneurs safely and effectively, I recommend: *Better Than a Lemonade Stand* by Daryl Bernstein and *The Totally Awesome Business Book* for Kids by Adriane G. Berg and Arthur Berg Bochner.

HOME-BASED TECHNOLOGY

Familiarizing your child with a calculator and a computer are ways that your child can become "technology literate" at home. Technology can be user-friendly to a child as young as three years old. Educational software can be categorized into two major categories: drill and practice and those that provide problem solving opportunities. Each day, more and more educational software hits the marketplace. Rather than give you a list of recommended software (as it would be outdated by the time this book is published), I recommend the following reputable software companies including: Broderbund, Davidson, Dorling Kindersley, Edmark, Tom Snyder, The Learning Company, Sunburst, Video Discovery, and Voyager.

When considering a specific piece of software, the following list of characteristics from *Bringing Out the Best* by Jacquelyn Saunders with Pamela Espeland will assist you in rating the software. Here are some tips:

- Animation. In an animated program, the figures and objects on the display terminal move, either on their own or when prompted by the child. Is the animation interesting, novel, meaningful, or just showy?

- Color. Some programs require a color monitor and children tend to prefer programs with color in them. Again, how is it used?

- Closure. Is an ending provided for the program or does it keep running until the child chooses to stop? Opinion is divided on which is best but we lean toward the former.

- Reinforcement. How is the child "rewarded" for correct responses? Some programs include sound, music, building a picture, animation, letting the child play a game, etc.

- Teaching/prompting. How does the program react to an incorrect response? Does it immediately provide the answer or give clues to help the child reach it on his or her own?

- Levels of difficulty and complexity. Will the program grow with your child?

When using this guide, rate each of these characteristics on a continuum from awful to excellent. The best guide of all would be for you and your child to try a demonstration at your local school, public library, or in the store before you buy it. If this is not possible, check the company's return and/or refund policy before you make a purchase.[1]

Some additional advice on interacting with your child in creating a positive mathematical environment comes from the book *Family Math* by Stenmark, Thompson, and Cossey:

- Let your children know that you believe they can succeed. Let them see you enjoying the activities, liking mathematics. Children tend to emulate their parents, and if a parent says "You know, this is really interesting!" that becomes the child's model.

- Be ready to talk with your children about mathematics and to listen to what they are saying. Even when you yourself don't know how to solve a problem, asking a child to explain the meaning of each part of the problem will probably be enough to find a strategy.

- Be more concerned with the processes of doing mathematics than with getting a correct answer. The answer to any particular problem has very little importance but knowing how to find the answer is a lifetime skill.

- Try not to tell children how to solve the problem. Once they have been told how to do it, thinking usually stops. Better to ask them questions about the problem and help them find their own methods of working it through.

- Practice estimation with your children whenever possible. Estimation helps the thinking about a problem that precedes the doing, and is one of the most useful and "sense-making" tools available.

- Provide a special place for study, allowing your child to help you gear the study environment to his or her learning style. Some kids really do work better sprawled on the floor or bed, or with a musical background. There are no hard and fast rules!

- Encourage group study. Open your home to informal study groups. Promote outside formal study groups related perhaps to scouts, church, or school organizations. This will be especially important as your children grow older.

- Expect that homework will be done. Look at the completed work regularly. But try to keep your comments positive. Don't become a drill sergeant. Praise your child for asking questions about the work. To be successful, your child will need to study 30-60 hours a week in college, at least an hour and a half each day in middle school, and probably 20 minutes a day in elementary grades. The experts

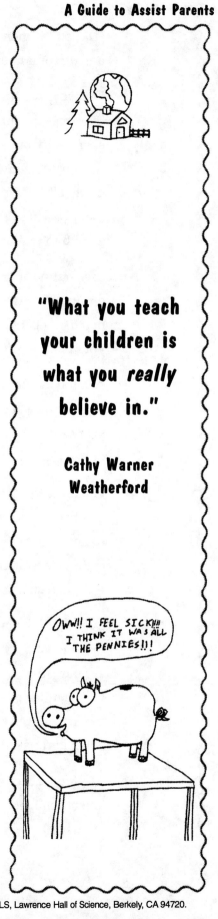

"What you teach your children is what you *really* believe in."

Cathy Warner
Weatherford

tell us that there is a high correlation between success in mathematics and the amount of homework done.

- Don't expect that all homework will be easy for your child or be disappointed that it seems difficult. Never indicate that you feel your child is stupid. This may sound silly but sometimes loving, caring parents unintentionally give their kids the most negative messages: for example, "Even your little sister, Stephanie, can do that," or "Hurry up, can't you see that the answer is ten?" or "Don't worry, math was hard for me, too. And, besides, you'll never use it!" or "How come you got a B in math when you could get A's in everything else?"

- Seek out positive ways to support your child's teacher and school. Join the parent group. Offer to help find materials or role models. Accompany field trips. Avoid making negative comments about the teacher or the school in front of your child; your child needs to maintain a good feeling about the school.

- Ask the teacher to give you a course outline or a list of the expectations for each class or subject of study. They should be available at the beginning of the school year or at a Back to School Night. These will help you know how your child is doing. [See Chapter 3 for a sample list of curriculum by grade level.]

- Find time to sit in on your child's classes. Go to school events such as Open House and Back to School Night. Volunteer during the school day in your child's classroom. (I personally recommend volunteering during the school day in your child's classroom. As a teacher I always appreciated the support that comes with parents learning about their child's classroom.)

- Look carefully at the standardized test results and ask about any test scores that may indicate a skill deficiency or a special talent. But do not use these test scores as your primary means of assessment. The teacher's observations and your own will be much more valuable. Some of the most important attributes, such as sticking with a problem or having many effective strategies to use, are not tested with paper and pencil.

- Ask the teacher at the beginning of the term how placement decisions are made for subsequent courses especially if your child is in the upper grades or is changing schools.

- Try not to drill your child on math content or create hostilities by insisting that math work be done at any one specific time or in a specific way. Don't use math work as punishment. Parents, adolescents, and children have enough things that may create friction without adding math to the list.

- Model persistence and pleasure with mathematics. Include enrichment, recreational mathematics in your family routine. Try to introduce math ideas (with a light touch!) at the dinner table, or while traveling, even to the grocery store.

- Above all, enjoy mathematics![2]

SUPPORTING YOUR CHILD'S MATH EXPLORATIONS AT SCHOOL

As with any subject, your child needs support from home in order to do his or her best in school. And, again, the old saw comes as no surprise: model that which you want your child to learn.

Parents As Teachers

To support your child's math explorations at school, it is critical that you and your family become math explorers, too. Also, you need to know enough about what your child is doing at school so you can help expand that learning through real-life experiences at home. The following are recommendations from the National Council of Teachers of Mathematics as listed in their brochure, "Help Your Child Learn Math":

- Do ask your child's teacher about the kinds of help that you as a parent can provide. Your role is to reinforce and help your child practice the things taught at school.

- Do encourage a child to restate what a mathematical word problem is all about—the information it gives and the information it asks for. Putting it in the child's own words will help clarify it.

- Do make sure that "home" math has a noticeable problem-solving flavor. It should contain a challenge or question that must be answered. (How many nickels do you have in your bank. How many do you need to buy an ice cream cone?)

- Do use objects that your child can touch, handle, and move. Researchers call these things "manipulatives." They can be any familiar objects such as soft toys, blocks, marbles, drinking straws, fruit, etc.

- Don't tell your child that some people are "no good" in math. Never tell your child you are "no good" in math no matter how low your opinion of your own skills may be.

- Don't think that girls aren't as good in math as boys.[3]

Setting Appropriate Expectations

Regardless of the age of your child, it is important for parents to hold expectations for their child(ren) that are both high and challenging yet age-appropriate. Depending on the age(s) of your child(ren), you may want to focus on particular concepts. Although each school or district may have its own list of particular mathematical skills to be learned at a specific grade level (or levels if your child is in a multi-age/multi-grade classroom), the following is a general list of the concepts generally covered in particular grade levels. This list has been reproduced from the book *Family Math* by Stenmark, Thompson, and Cossey. If you would like further information, please consult your child's teacher.

Good Luck!!!

"It is okay to fail, but it is not okay to give up."

Kate, age 8

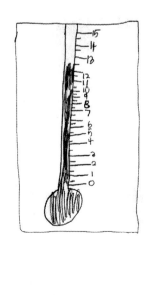

MATHEMATICS GENERALLY COVERED IN KINDERGARTEN

Applications

- Talking about mathematics used in our daily lives

Numbers

- Learning to estimate how many

- Counting objects, up to about 15 or 20

- Putting out objects to match a number

- Comparing two sets of objects

- Recognizing numerals up to 20

- Writing numerals, 0 through 9

- Learning about ordinal numbers, such as first, second, third

Measurement

- Estimating and comparing:

    taller or shorter

    longer or shorter

    largest or smallest

    heavier or lighter

Geometry

- Recognizing and classifying colors and simple shapes

Patterns

- Recognizing simple patterns, continuing them, and making up new patterns

Probability and Statistics

- Making and talking about simple graphs of everyday things, such as birthdays, pets, food, and so on

MATHEMATICS GENERALLY COVERED IN FIRST GRADE

Applications

- Talking about mathematics used in daily living

- Learning strategies such as using manipulatives or drawing diagrams to solve problems.

Arithmetic and Numbers

- Practicing estimating skills

- Counting through about 100

- Recognizing, writing, and being able to order numbers through about 100

- Counting by twos, fives, and tens

- Using ordinal numbers, such as first, second, tenth, and so on

- Learning basic addition and subtraction facts up to 9+9=18 and 18-9=9

- Developing understanding of place value using tens and ones with manipulatives, including base ten blocks, Cuisenaire rods, abaci, play money, and so on

- Developing the concept of fractional values such as halves, thirds, and fourths

Measurement

- Telling time to the hour or half-hour (but don't press it not mastered)

- Recognizing and using calendars, days of the week, months

- Estimating lengths and measuring things with non-standard units, such as how many handprints across the table

- Understanding uses and relative values of pennies, nickels, dimes

Geometry and Patterns

- Working with shapes, such as triangles, circles, squares, rectangles

- Recognizing, repeating, and making up geometric and numeric patterns

Probability and Statistics

- Making and interpreting simple graphs, using blocks or people, of everyday things, such as color preferences, number of brothers and sisters, and so on

MATHEMATICS GENERALLY COVERED IN SECOND GRADE

Applications

- Talking about mathematics used in daily life

- Creating and solving word problems in measurement, geometry, probability, and statistics, as well as arithmetic

- Practicing strategies for solving problems, such as drawing diagrams, organized guessing, putting problems into own words, and so on

Numbers

- Practicing estimation skills

- Reading and writing numbers through about 1,000, playing around with up to 10,000

- Counting by twos, fives, and tens, and maybe some other numbers for fun

- Learning about odd and even numbers

- Using ordinal numbers such as first, second, tenth

- Identifying fractions such as halves, thirds, quarters

- Understanding and using the signs for greater than (>) and less than (<)

Arithmetic

- Knowing addition and subtraction facts through 9+9=18 and 18-9=9

- Estimating answers to other addition and subtraction problems

- Practicing addition and subtraction with and without regrouping (carrying), such as:

27	27	27	27
+2	+8	-2	-8
29	35	25	19

- Adding columns of numbers, such as

2
8
9
+7

- Exploring uses of a calculator

- Being introduced to multiplication and division

Geometry

- Finding congruent shapes (same size and shape)

- Recognizing and naming squares, rectangles, circles, and maybe some other polygons

- Informally recognizing lines of symmetry

- Reading and drawing very simple maps

Measurement

- Practicing estimation of measurements—how many toothpicks long is the table?

- Comparing lengths, areas, weights

- Measuring with non-standard units, beginning to use some standard units such as inches or centimeters

- Telling time to the nearest quarter-hour, maybe to the minute

- Making change with coins and bills, doing money problems with manipulatives

- Knowing days of the week and months, and using the calendar to find dates

Probability and Statistics

- Making and interpreting simple graphs, using physical objects or manipulatives

- Doing simple probability activities

Patterns

- Working with patterns of numbers, shapes, colors, sounds, and so on, including adding to existing patterns, completing missing sections, making up new patterns

MATHEMATICS GENERALLY COVERED IN THIRD GRADE

Applications

- Talking about mathematics seen in students' lives

- Creating, analyzing, and solving word problems in all of the concept areas

- Practicing a variety of problem-solving strategies with problems of more than one step

Numbers

- Practicing estimation skills with all problems

- Reading and writing numbers through about 10,000, exploring those beyond 10,000

- Counting by twos, threes, fours, fives and tens and other numbers

- Naming and comparing fractions such as 1/2 is greater than 1/4

- Identifying fractions of a whole number such as 1/2 of 12 is 6

- Exploring concepts of decimal numbers such as tenths and hundredths, using money to represent values

- Using the signs for greater than (>) and less than (<)

Arithmetic

- Learning how to use calculators effectively

- Using calculators to solve problems

- Continuing to practice basic addition and subtraction facts and simple addition and subtraction problems

- Doing larger and more complicated addition and subtraction problems

$$\begin{array}{r} 3897 \\ +8342 \end{array} \qquad \begin{array}{r} 8342 \\ -3897 \end{array}$$

- Beginning to learn multiplication and division facts through 9x9=81 and 81 divided by 9 = 9

- Beginning to learn multiplication and division of two- and three-digit numbers by a single-digit number

    27   124

    <u>X3</u>   <u>X 8</u>   <u>6/24</u>

- Learning about remainders

    4R1

    7/29

    28

    1

Geometry

- Recognizing and naming shapes such as squares, rectangles, trapezoids, triangles, circles, and three-dimensional objects such as cubes, cylinders, and the like

- Identifying congruent shapes (same size and shape)

- Recognizing lines of symmetry, and reflections (mirror images) and translations (movements to a different position) of figures

- Reading and drawing simple maps, using coordinates

- Learning about parallel (| |) and perpendicular (⊥) lines

Measurement

- Estimating before doing measurements

- Using non-standard and some standard units to measure:

- Length (toothpicks, straws, paper strips, string lengths, and so on)

    (centimeters, decimeters, meters, inches, feet, yards)

- Perimeters (same as length)

- Area   (square units) (paper squares, tiles, and so on)
    (square centimeters, meters, inches, feet, yards)

- Weight (paper clips, rocks, blocks, beans, and so on)
    (grams, kilograms, ounces, pounds)

- Volume and capacity (blocks, rice, beans, water; in cans, paper cups, and so on)
    (liters, cubic centimeters, cups, gallons, pints, quarts)

- Temperature (° Celsius, ° Fahrenheit)

- Telling time, probably to the nearest minute

- Continuing to use money to develop understanding of decimals

- Using calendars

Probability and Statistics

- Being introduced to probability concepts, such as the chance of something happening

- Using tally marks, collecting and organizing informal data

- Making, reading, and interpreting simple graphs

Patterns

- Continuing to work with patterns, including those found on addition and multiplication charts

MATHEMATICS GENERALLY COVERED IN FOURTH GRADE

Applications

- Talking about uses of mathematics in students' lives and in their futures

- Creating, analyzing, and solving word problems in all of the concept areas

- Using a variety of problem-solving strategies to solve problems with multiple steps

- Working in groups to solve complex problems

- Using calculators for problem-solving

- Developing formal and informal mathematical vocabulary

Numbers and Operations

- Practicing rounding and estimation skills with all problems

- Using calculators with some proficiency for all operations

- Reading and writing numbers to 10,000 and beyond

- Learning about special numbers, such as primes, factors, multiples, square numbers

- Recognizing equivalent fractions, such as 1/2=2/4

- Finding fractions of whole numbers, such as 1/8 of 72=9

- Maintaining and extending work with the operations of addition, subtraction, multiplication, and division of whole numbers

- Adding and subtracting simple decimal numbers

- Learning about simple percents such as 10%, 50%, and 100%

Geometry

- Using geometric shapes to find patterns of corners, diagonals, edges, and so on

- Recognizing right angles, exploring terminology of other angles

- Continuing to explore ideas connected with symmetry

- Reading and drawing simple maps, using coordinates

- Exploring terminology and uses of coordinate grid

- Identifying parallel (| |) and perpendicular (⊥) lines

- Exploring how different shapes fill a flat surface (tiling)

Measurement

- Estimating before measuring

- Using non-standard and standard units to measure length, area, volume, weight, temperature

- Telling time for a purpose

- Making simple scale drawings

- Exploring terminology and uses of geometric grid

Probability and Statistics

- Using sampling techniques to collect information or conduct a survey

- Discussing uses and meanings of statistics, such as how to make a survey fair, how to show the most information, how to find averages

- Making, reading, and interpreting graphs

- Performing simple probability experiments, discussing results

MATHEMATICS GENERALLY COVERED IN FIFTH AND SIXTH GRADES

Applications

- Talking about mathematics used in present and future lives

- Creating, analyzing, and solving word problems in all of the concept areas

- Using a variety of problem solving strategies to solve problems with multiple steps

- Working in groups to solve complex problems

- Using calculators for problem solving

- Developing mathematical vocabulary

Numbers and Arithmetic

- Practicing rounding and estimation skills with all problems

- Using calculators effectively for appropriate problems

- Expanding understanding and use of special numbers such as primes, composite numbers, square and cubic numbers, common divisors, common multiples

- Increasing understanding of fraction relationships:

    comparisons, such as $2/3 > 1/2$

    equivalence, such as $2/3 = 4/6$

    reducing, such as $10/20 = 1/2$

    relating mixed numbers and improper fractions, such as $2\ 1/3 = 7/3$

- Developing skills in adding, subtracting, multiplying, dividing fractions (mastery not expected)

- Maintaining skills in basic addition, subtraction, multiplication, division of whole numbers

- Adding, subtracting, multiplying, and dividing decimal numbers

- Computing percents, and relating percents to fractions and decimals

- Developing some understanding of ratio and proportion

- Exploring scientific notation such as $3 \times 108 = 300{,}000{,}000$

Geometry

- Using the concept of parallel (| |) and perpendicular (⊥) lines
- Measuring and drawing angles of various kinds
- Understanding circle relationships, including diameter, circumference, radius
- Recognizing shapes that are congruent, or the same size and shape
- Recognizing shapes that are similar, or the same shape but a different size
- Developing understanding of symmetry, reflections, and translations of figures
- Drawing constructions such as equal line segments or perpendicular bisectors
- Understanding coordinate graphing
- Drawing and reading maps
- Doing perspective drawing

Measurement

- Continuing to use hands-on tools of measurement, estimating first in all cases, for:

    length

    area

    volume and capacity

    mass or weight

    temperature — celsius and fahrenheit

    telling time accurately

Probability and Statistics

- Performing and reporting on a variety of probability experiments

- Collecting and organizing data

- Displaying data in graphic form, such as bar, picture, circle, line, and other graphs

- Beginning to develop understanding of statistical ideas such as mean, median, and mode

MATHEMATICS GENERALLY COVERED IN SEVENTH AND EIGHTH GRADES

Applications

- Talking about uses of mathematics and its importance to students' present and future lives (especially important for female and minority students)

- Creating, analyzing, and solving word problems in all of the concept areas

- Using a variety of problem solving strategies to solve problems with multiple steps

- Working in groups to solve complex problems

- Using calculators for problem solving

- Developing mathematical vocabulary

Numbers and Arithmetic

- Practicing rounding and estimation skills with all problems

- Using calculators with proficiency for appropriate problems

- Expanding understanding and use of special numbers such as primes, composite numbers, square and cubic numbers, common divisors, common multiples

- Increasing understanding of fraction relationships:

    comparisons, such as $2/3 > 1/2$

    equivalence, such as $2/3 = 4/6$

    reducing, such as $10/20 = 1/2$

    relating mixed numbers and improper fractions, such as $2\,1/3 = 7/3$

- Adding, subtracting, multiplying, and dividing fractions

- Adding, subtracting, multiplying, and dividing decimal numbers

- Maintaining skills in basic addition, subtraction, multiplication, division of whole numbers

- Computing percents, and relating percents to fractions and decimals

- Understanding of ratio and proportion

- Using scientific notation such as $3\times108 = 300,000,000$

- Learning about positive and negative numbers

- Finding greatest common factors (GCF) and least common multiples (LCM)

- Finding square roots

- Learning about special number relationships such as 2/5 is a reciprocal of 5/2

Geometry

- Using the concept of parallel (| |) and perpendicular (⊥) lines

- Measuring and drawing angles of various kinds

- Understanding circle relationships, including diameter, circumference, radius

- Using correct formulas to calculate areas of rectangles, triangles, circles, and so on

- Recognizing shapes that are congruent, or the same size and shape

- Recognizing shapes that are similar, or the same shape but a different size

- Developing understanding of symmetry, reflections, and translations of figures

- Making constructions such as equal line segments or perpendicular bisectors

- Understanding coordinate graphing

- Drawing and reading maps

- Doing perspective drawing

Measurement

- Continuing to use hands-on experiences with the tools of measurement, estimating first in all cases, for:

length	area
volume and capacity	mass or weight
temperature—celsius and fahrenheit	telling time accurately

Probability and Statistics

- Performing and reporting on a variety of probability experiments

- Collecting and organizing data

- Displaying data in graphic form, such as bar, picture, circle, line, and other graphs

- Beginning to develop understanding of statistical ideas such as mean, median, and mode

It's Not About Math, It's About Life

by Kari Simmons Kling

Published and Distributed by Books For Educators, Inc.

17051 SE 272nd Street, Suite 18

Kent, WA 98042-4959

253/630-6908   Fax 253/630-7215

www.books4educ.com

For Further Study

Family Math by Stenmark, Thompson, and Cossey

Math for the Very Young by Polonsky, Freedman, Lesher, and Morrison

Chapter 14
Assessment:

Authentic? . . . Performance? . . . Alternative?

What in the world are we talking about this time?

Given the volumes upon volumes of books and articles written about assessment and evaluation of every kind imaginable, it is not surprising to find that we do not speak the same language about assessment and evaluation, nor clearly see the big picture of assessment as an extension of classroom curriculum and a guide to day-to-day instructional planning. Recently, I interviewed twenty-five teachers and administrators about the differences between assessment, portfolios, and evaluation, and you guessed it, I received fifteen different responses. Do we truly know where we're going with this issue at hand?

We are all aware of the fact that we must get away from relying so heavily upon assessing what our students know on the basis of standardized, multiple-choice tests. The reasons are numerous. The most persuasive argument is that results from a standardized test at the end of the year provide no guidance for day-to-day instructional planning in the 100+ days prior to the test. Other assessment procedures and instruments are needed for daily assessment of "what students already know and need to know next." This is the kind of information useful to and needed by teachers as they plan from day to day. This chapter addresses this issue.

"Education is what you have left over after you have forgotten everything you've learned."

Anonymous

"History is more than dates. Literature is more than names of famous authors. And mathematics is more than 2+2 = 4. But mathematics assessment seems to be unable to move beyond this abysmally low level of sophistication: it's still about choosing the one correct answer."

Judah L. Schwartz

A second reason to avoid heavy reliance on standardized tests (which usually involves misusing the tests and their results) is that they encourage teaching to the test. Two mistakes appear here: standardized tests (because of time restraints) represent a limited view of mathematics and real-world applications beyond arithmetic functions. Furthermore, the format of the tests (dictated by the economics of scoring methods for mass testing) are artificial and close-ended—true/false or multiple choice responses in which the correct answer is present and guessing is rampant. As a result, says Lorrie Shepard, "teaching to the test" is forced even on those teachers that don't want to do it and it "cheapens instruction and . . . undermines the authenticity of scores as measures of what children really know. The more we focus on raising test scores, the more instruction is distorted, and the less credible are the scores themselves."[1]

It is not that we shouldn't be accountable to ourselves and our communities but the majority of "test scores" are not an accurate account of what our students can do with the information being assessed. Being able to find the correct answer to a computation problem does not provide a direct correlation to whether students know when and how to apply that skill beyond the walls of the classroom.

"We test students for what they recognize rather than what they understand. Yet these kinds of skills have little or no relevance beyond school walls. Individuals outside of the classroom are rarely, if ever, asked to diagram sentences, draw a color wheel, complete an isolated analogy, or fill in missing pieces of a mathematical formula. Instead, they are expected to pursue projects over time, to collaborate and converse with others, to take responsibility for their work, provoking and engaging in reflection and revision, and to amplify their understandings and apply them in powerful ways or in new or surprising contexts. If assessment is to be a moment in an educational process rather than simply an evaluative vehicle, then it must be seen and used as an opportunity to develop complex understandings."[2]

True accountability should revolve around the twin issues of being responsible for what we teach and how much of it students learn from us. In contrast, standardized tests ask "do you know, in this format, what I think you should know." And a random, disjointed bunch of stuff it is!

These are very real and very disturbing problems. We need the means of keeping ourselves accountable that don't distort our efforts to enhance math understandings and the ability to apply them to the real world.

ADDING A DAB OF COMMON SENSE

As bandied about the educational field, assessment and evaluation are complex issues, so complex that we usually lose our common sense somewhere among the rabbit warren passages that we follow in search of useful, useable answers. In Susan Kovalik's mind, however, there are two common sense questions:

> **What do you want students to understand?** *(not just recognize)*
> ### AND
> **What do you want them to do with it?** *(in terms of real world applications)*

Simple and to the point: the answer to every parent's dream for their child and the focus every teacher searches for when attempting to integrate content.

Assessment and Evaluation in the Kovalik ITI Model

Within Kovalik's ITI Model is a step-by-step discussion of how to create instruments and processes for daily use in assessing progress and planning the next lesson. It is the best advice I know of. Kovalik recommends using the structure of daily activities or inquiries as the basis for assessment. Her model describes how to construct such real-world activities and then how to convert them into powerful and reliable assessment tools.

The standards or criteria for judging performance on such activities involve common sense areas. Called the 4 C's of assessment, the essential questions ask if the performance is correct, complete, comprehensive, and connected to the real world (that is, the task is one that adults would face in daily living and thus is worthy of students' time).

For more information, see the chapters on assessment in any of the following books: *ITI: The Model* by Susan Kovalik, *Kid's Eye View of Science: A Teacher's Handbook for Implementing an Integrated Approach to Teaching Science, K-6* by S. Kovalik and Karen Olsen, or *The Way We Were . . . The Way We CAN Be: A Vision for the Middle School* by Ann Ross and K. Olsen.

Useful Perspectives for Creating Your Own Assessment System

So, how are new assessment practices moving away from conventional practices? Edward Chittenden points out some of these differences in strategies in his article, "Authentic Assessment, Evaluation, and Documentation of Student Performance." He compares the new and conventional practices as follows:[3]

New assessment practices:
- are ongoing, cumulative
- use open-ended formats
- draw upon a variety of settings
- are theory-referenced
- are teacher-mediated

Conventional practices are:
- annual
- multiple-choice
- based on single setting
- norm-referenced
- teacher-proof

In 1992, ASCD issued a book entitled, *A Practical Guide to Alternative Assessment*, written by Herman, Aschbacher, and Winters.[4] The authors provide the following advice which is based on decades of measurement research and followed, with certain variations, by developers of high-quality tests, be they norm-referenced, criterion-referenced, or performance-based tests.

- Specify the nature of the skills and accomplishments students are to develop.

- Specify illustrative tasks that would require students to demonstrate these skills and accomplishments.

- Specify the criteria and standards for judging student performance on the task.

- Develop a reliable rating process.

- Gather evidence of validity to show what kinds of inferences can be made from the assessment.

- Use test results to refine assessment and improve curriculum and instruction; provide feedback to students, parents, and the community.

Herman, J.L., Ascbacher, P.R., & Winters, L. The National Center for Research on Evaluation, Standards and Student Testing (CRESST). *A Practical Guide To Alternative Assessment.* Alexandria, VA: ASCD. © 1992 by the Regents of the University of California.

It is crucial to ensure that assessment is not done in isolation of its real-world applications of the skills and knowledge to be assessed; it should always occur with clear outcomes in mind and preferably after a student has had an opportunity to engage in a "being there" experience which gives context and relevance to the math concepts to be learned. **Remember, it's not about math; it's about life!**

Is Your Curriculum Friend or Foe?

Keen assessment does not happen in a vacuum, in isolation from the application of the skills and concepts being evaluated. The most important aspect of good assessment is the integration of effective teaching and learning, an integral part of good instruction. The everyday classroom environment should be able to provide teachers with opportunities to assess what their students know and to show what they can do with it. This is a natural process when the curriculum is student-driven, meaningful, and relevant to the child's real world. But—and it is a big but—"you can't have authentic assessment without authentic curriculum."[5] Designing good assessment and evaluation instruments and processes must often begin with redesign of the curriculum to be assessed.

For assistance in analyzing your district's math curriculum, see Chapters 3 and 4, What Is Math? and Language and Math.

As discussed in Chapter 8, Integrating Math: The Final Frontier, an effective mathematics program is a blend of skillshops that ensure basic math skills and real-world applications of math through finding math in "being there" experiences, integrating math into your curriculum, etc.

TOWARD A COMPREHENSIVE VIEW OF MATH EVALUATION

One of the most frequently asked question is "What does a comprehensive math evaluation system look like in action?" The following description developed out of a school I taught at. It's a beginning point from which to design a system appropriate for your school. The mindmap on the next page is a useful tool for summarizing how teachers are evaluating the math progress of students and for communicating to parents how both basic math skills and the concepts of mathematics are being addressed and assessed.

Initial Assessment

Among the first things you want to know about your class is what each child has mastered (understands and knows how to apply in real-world settings), what each

MATH ASSESSMENT AND EVALUATION

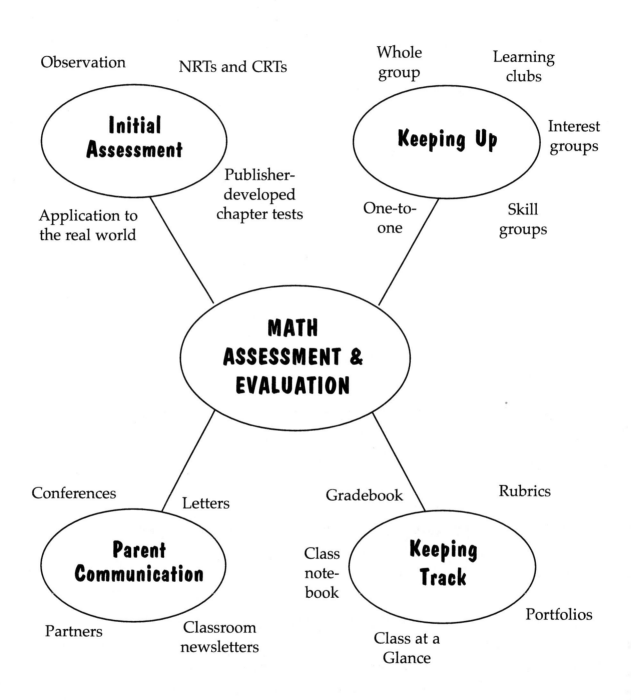

Observation · NRTs and CRTs · Whole group · Learning clubs

Initial Assessment · **Keeping Up**

Interest groups

Application to the real world · Publisher-developed chapter tests · One-to-one · Skill groups

MATH ASSESSMENT & EVALUATION

Conferences · Letters · Gradebook · Rubrics

Parent Communication · Class notebook · **Keeping Track**

Partners · Classroom newsletters · Class at a Glance · Portfolios

For a discussion of each of these areas, see pages 14.7-18.

understands but has not learned to apply in real-world settings, what each can recognize but not understand, and what each has so little experience with that they do not even recognize. After this the teacher can begin to organize the teaching of math concepts (through such approaches as theme math and "being there" experiences) and Skillshops (and other means of meeting students' individual needs without holding back the rest of the class). Basic skills can then be taught to the whole group (everyone needs to learn this skill), to a small group, or to an individual (only this student needs this skill). **Note:** The tools and processes for initial assessment are the same for on-going assessment, only the timeline varies.

Observation. Yetta Goodman always refers to the student observer as the "kid watcher." Many times some of the most useful data that we can gather about what a child does and does not know is simply by observing and taking anecdotal notes as we go. There are many ways to organize these observations and I encourage you to do whatever works for you. I chose to record my observation on labels that I carried on a clipboard. Each label represented a separate observation, the student's name, date, and what the child did. When I had a spare moment, I simply peeled off the label and stuck it in child's record folder.

Observation-based assessments are very useful throughout the year, during any kind of activity, and for assessing any math concept and skill. They should be ongoing. Examples of opportunities for observation-based assessment include:

- student-generated story problems: based on experience and current skill(s), knowledge, or concept being studied

- independent work time: nature of math activities, games, computer programs

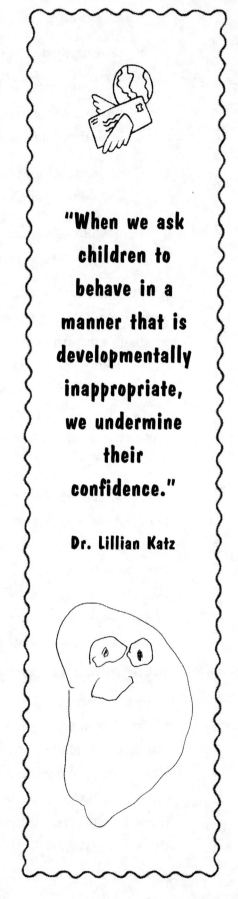

"When we ask children to behave in a manner that is developmentally inappropriate, we undermine their confidence."

Dr. Lillian Katz

- skill groups: computational strategies, various problem-solving capabilities

- reading related: incorporating mathematical concepts within literature, nonfiction, newspaper articles, etc.

- writing: use of math journals, stories, vocabulary, incorporation of math concepts into stories, research

- informal settings: use of mathematical concepts, vocabulary and computation in everyday settings, e.g., going to the store, counting money, telling time, etc.

- use of resources: student knows when and how to use a calculator and/or computer appropriately[6]

NRT's & CRT's. Every school has some kind of state, district, and/or school norm-referenced testing (NRT) or standardized test that must be done at the beginning of the year for diagnostic purposes. (The purposes vary from test to test, state to state, and district to district.) Since you have to give these tests anyway, use, but don't abuse, them as another source for you to gain information about a given student. However, for initial and ongoing day-to-day instructional planning purposes, you may want to give your own type of pretest based on skills, interest, or specific knowledge relating to your content (criterion-referenced tests or CRT).

Publisher-developed chapter tests. Although I didn't use a math textbook, I still administered the end of the chapter tests from the adopted math text of my district to my students. Even though I knew that my students were "getting the skills," I had to be accountable to their parents, other teachers, my principal, and my school district. So, periodically, in addition to all of the other accountability issues explored in this section, I gave the end-of-the-chapter tests from the text. These scores were kept in my grade book and were used as "part of the mix" of information about my students accomplishments in math.

Application to the real world. Using a combination of classroom observations and test results, I can begin to find out what I most want to know: can a student apply the skills to real-life, problem-solving situations. If a child can answer a question about multiplication on a test but can't compute the money he or she has in his or her hand, I know that mastery has not occurred. I want to focus on the application of a particular skill instead of just having the knowledge. To me as a teacher, the two most important assessment questions are: **What do you want the students to understand** and **What do you want them to do with it?** The student must know what to do with it!

Keeping Up

Initial assessment gives you clues about where to begin and how to proceed but as the year progresses, you will need to rely more and more upon observation of students against clearly defined math concepts and skills. Keeping up with student growth requires great flexibility in instructional planning and student grouping practices.

Changes in grouping need to occur for a variety of reasons: the nature of the "being there" experience to illustrate use of the math concept, the content of the task for group work, the skill(s) to be worked on, and the interest of the student(s).

Whole group. Despite the rhetoric, and the genuine need for individualizing instruction, there is still a place for whole class instruction, particularly during theme math, "being there" experiences, and other means of providing students experience with the real-world application of math concepts. A great deal of your direct instruction may be geared to the entire class.

Learning clubs. Once you have delivered your direct instruction, students may extend the lesson while working collaboratively in their cooperative learning groups, developing and extending what was just introduced. Learning clubs (collaborative learning groups) generally are the workhorse of your math instruction as they allow students to explore and share their learnings, particularly during the time dedicated to practice applying what they are learning to real-world situations.

Interest groups. Depending on what is being studied, students may choose which group they might like to be in based on interest. For example, when teaching about graphs, you may have four groups of students working on different aspects of graphs, e.g., how graphs are used to communicate information in the newspapers, how to use graphs as a persuasive tool in advertising, how to create graphs from student collected data, and, lastly, how to use graphs to compare and contrast information. Each group could research and present their findings to members of the other groups. Likewise, each group could be assigned a different kind of graph to represent specified data. Sharing could focus on analyzing which format best illustrates the relevant information.

The possibilities are endless but the key ingredient is that the assignment is of genuine interest to students, i.e., the work is student generated, not teacher driven.

Skill groups. Membership in skill groups changes weekly, even daily, as does the skill to be worked on. (As a rule of thumb, no group should remain unchanged for more than three weeks.) Simply gather those students to work on that skill while the rest of the class may be involved in other small group projects, independent practice, or a research project. Don't forget about using parent helpers, peer tutoring, or buddy tutors from an upper grade class to assist you in the management of this.

One-to-one. Some students work best as a group of one, preferring to work alone. Other students may need greater mediation—explanation of the relevant aspects of a pattern in math that he or she will best relate to—and thus need you on a one-on-one basis. This can be easily arranged during "buddy work" time, an assignment directing students to work in pairs. This would be an ideal time for you to be that particular student's buddy.

However, don't always choose the same "buddy." Rotate yourself around the room on different days. Another way to have one-on-one time is while the rest of the class is working independently or in small groups. I also recommend working with individual students before or after school if time allows. Groupings and their assigned content should never be fixed but should be ongoing and ever changing.

Keeping Track

Keeping track of student growth requires a variety of management strategies. Here are just a few that I have found to be very helpful.

Grade book. Methods for how and what grades are recorded in the formal grade book vary. Districts or states often dictate a specific format. Districts may dictate what gets graded and how. Many of you are required to keep letter or number grades even though many educators are desperately trying to do away with giving letter or number grades. Here's a suggestion: As stated earlier, Kovalik recommends that "grading" be looked at as "the 4C's of assessment." Is the information correct, complete (was the criteria met?), is it comprehensive (does it reflect more than one point of view?), and does it connect to real life (is the assigned problem to be solved placed in a real-world context?). If you must give a grade, you can then convert the 4C's into a judgment of mastered or not mastered. All unmastered work thus remains as work yet to be done, not failure.

The importance of this perspective is that it eliminates the grading of individual classroom or homework assignments or tests with letter grades (which may or may not have anything to do with whether a concept or skill has been learned) and places the focus of the grade book upon identified concepts and skills (and whether they have been mastered or not yet mastered). Thus, how many assignments or tests a student may undertake is unimportant; what is important is whether mastery occurs—the ability to use the math concept or skill in real-world settings and store it in long-term memory.

For a simple but useful grade book format, see "Class at a Glance," on page 14.15.

Rubrics. Rubric formats are another way to avoid letter grades and at the same time pro-vide information useful for focusing day-to-day instructional planning. Whether there are three, four, five, or a dozen stages, it is up to you to define what the criteria will be.

Rubrics, homemade or adopted or adapted, are a useful tool to help the student move toward mastery. On the next two pages are examples from Denise Zimmerer, a multiage teacher (grades 1 and 2) in Phoenix, Arizona, of a rubric for math and a means of record-ing student progress. Denise uses the rubric to help her assess her students' areas of strength and those areas that need further development. The rubric was developed using the sample rubric from *Puddle Questions Series* and assessment guidelines from *Making Connections: Teaching and the Human Brain*, by Renate and Geoffrey Caine.

I have also found Caines' assessment guidelines valuable when pushing myself to create real-world contexts for math problems and especially when trying to judge whether or not a student has finally developed a mental program for using a concept or skill in the future (the learning has been wired into the student's long-term memory). The guidelines are:[7]

- The ability to use the language of the discipline or subject in complex situations and in social interaction.

- The ability to perform appropriately in unanticipated situations.

- The ability to solve real problems using the skills and concepts.

- The ability to show, explain, or teach the idea or skill to another person who has a real need to know.

Portfolios. In 1991 the National Council of Teachers of Mathematics published a book entitled *Mathematics Assessment: Myths, Models, Good Questions, and Practical Suggestions.* According to the authors, a portfolio is "a showcase for student work, a place where many types of assignments, projects, reports, and writings can be collected." Other comments listed in favor of portfolios include:

- The students become part of the system and can see their own progress.

- The student and the teacher can discuss (orally or in writing) strengths, areas for improvement, likes, and dislikes. Dialog between teacher and student, in either conversation or a journal, is important for the portfolio process.
- The student, teacher, and parents can sit down together and talk about what is in the portfolio, what mathematics means for the student, and the progress being made in the subject.

SCORING RUBRIC

Low Feedback: Level 1 (score of 1)

Demonstrates confusion about key point or problem.

No transfer of knowledge from one area to another independently.

Difficulty solving real problems using the skills and concepts taught.

Student feedback has significant flaws.

Project/task result is communicated poorly, lacks related vocabulary, completeness, and organization.

Unable to relate thinking/reasoning/procedures to others.

Medium Feedback: Level 2 (score of 2)

Demonstrates some comprehension of the key point or problem.

Slight transfer of knowledge from one area to another independently.

Some evidence of solving real problems using the skills and concepts taught.

Contains the components of required task response but lacks detail and depth.

Project/task result is communicated poorly, lacks related vocabulary, completeness and organization.

Able to explain thinking satisfactorily but lacks important details.

High Feedback: Level 3 (score of 3)

Demonstrates significant understanding of the key point or problem.

Evidence of transfer of knowledge from one area to another independently.

Little difficulty solving real problems using the skills and concepts taught.

Feedback shows details and depth.

Project/task result is communicated clearly, using related vocabulary, shows organization, completeness, and some originality.

Remarkable Feedback: Level 4 (score of 4)

Demonstrates high feedback level with ease.

Has added additional details to demonstrate knowledge without being asked.

Feedback is innovative.

Able to provide strong supporting information without difficulty.

Level of thinking and task vocabulary is beyond what is expected for students at this particular time for the particular project/task.

General Assessment Recording Form

Quarter:

Area:

*See assessment scoring rubric for math

Low Feedback: Level 1 (score 1)

Medium Feedback: Level 2 (score 2)

High Feedback: Level 3 (score 3)

Remarkable Feedback: Level 4 (score 4)

last. first	St. ID	DATE / SKILL	DATE / SKILL	DATE / SKILL						Observation Final Grade

Assessment

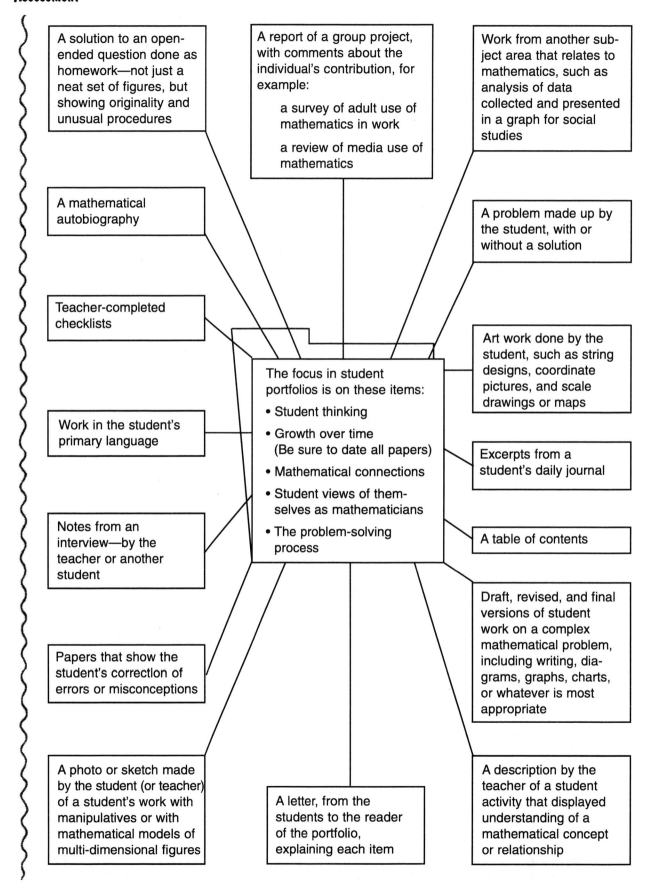

A solution to an open-ended question done as homework—not just a neat set of figures, but showing originality and unusual procedures

A report of a group project, with comments about the individual's contribution, for example:

a survey of adult use of mathematics in work

a review of media use of mathematics

Work from another subject area that relates to mathematics, such as analysis of data collected and presented in a graph for social studies

A mathematical autobiography

A problem made up by the student, with or without a solution

Teacher-completed checklists

Art work done by the student, such as string designs, coordinate pictures, and scale drawings or maps

Work in the student's primary language

The focus in student portfolios is on these items:
• Student thinking
• Growth over time (Be sure to date all papers)
• Mathematical connections
• Student views of themselves as mathematicians
• The problem-solving process

Excerpts from a student's daily journal

A table of contents

Notes from an interview—by the teacher or another student

Draft, revised, and final versions of student work on a complex mathematical problem, including writing, diagrams, graphs, charts, or whatever is most appropriate

Papers that show the student's correction of errors or misconceptions

A photo or sketch made by the student (or teacher) of a student's work with manipulatives or with mathematical models of multi-dimensional figures

A letter, from the students to the reader of the portfolio, explaining each item

A description by the teacher of a student activity that displayed understanding of a mathematical concept or relationship

- Having students take portfolios home now and then can open communication and understanding for parents. Improvement over time can be illustrated and can be a beginning of discussion in conferences.

- School district officials can see the portfolio approach as a window into the program and as a growing assessment of the students and of the curriculum.

"Class at a glance." Tracking math achievement of specific skills and concepts by individual students can become bogged down if your recording format is cumbersome. I kept track of skills by using a form called a Class at a Glance (see example on page 4.15). When my students had truly mastered a basic skill in mathematics to the level of developing a mental program for long-term memory, I would either collect the paper that demonstrated this knowledge, take a photo of what had been done, or simply document what the child had done by writing an anecdotal note about it. It is important to always date each piece of documentation. As I collected this data, I would simply put the information in a basket on my desk. Approximately once every month or so, when the basket began to fill up, I "checked off" the appropriate box next to the student's name. Then, the corresponding documentation would be placed in that child's portfolio. This way everything that had been "checked off" had a cross-reference. You may be asking yourself how much time it took to complete this task. On average, approximately two hours each time I completed the update for the class. A small price to pay for such accountability! This provided me with such useful information when lesson planning!

"There is no such thing as a standardized kid."

David Lazear

Assessment

Class at a Glance

Individual math concepts and skills

Name of student										
1										
2										
3										
4										
5										
6										
7										
8										
9										
10										
11										
12										
13										
14										
15										
16										
17										
18										
19										
20										
21										
22										
23										
24										
25										
26										
27										
28										
29										
30										
31										
32										
33										
34										
35										

Teacher _____   Subject _____   Grade _____   Date _____

Class notebook. Using a three-ringed binder, with a divider for each child, is another useful tool in effective record keeping. The binder is the place to put the labels created when recording anecdotal records of student observations. In addition to the labels, this is a helpful place to record notes about parent conversations, conferences, or any other information about that particular child.

PARENT COMMUNICATION

Methods for maintaining ongoing communication of information about their child's progress is critical to parents. Some tried and true ways include the following.

Conferences. One way to do this is through parent, teacher, student conferences. I recommend that students lead these conferences, with your guidance. Even first graders can take an active role in explaining to parents their work and what they've learned. Don't forget to teach your students the necessary skills for leading a conference. Lots of role play is valuable.

Letters. Having students periodically write letters home about what they're doing is a useful tool for getting students to reflect on what they've done and where they're going. (The letters themselves are a demonstration of progress in writing skills.) Letters should be reviewed by the parent and signed. This letter can then go into the child's portfolio for documentation purposes.

Classroom newsletters. Monthly classroom newsletters with articles by the teacher and the students can communicate which skills will be highlighted during the month and can include questions that parents may want to ask their child about specific skills because sometimes parents do not know what to ask.

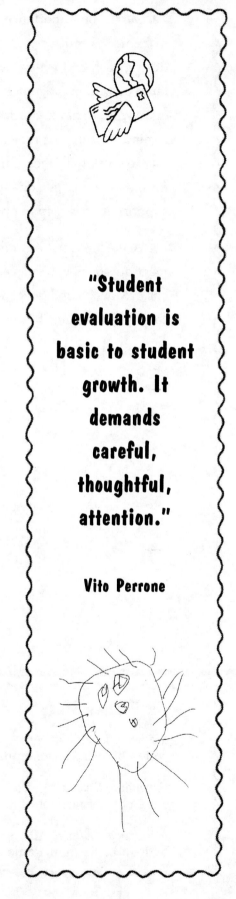

"Student evaluation is basic to student growth. It demands careful, thoughtful, attention."

Vito Perrone

Partners. The importance of the partnership between the parent and teacher cannot be overemphasized. From my very first letter on the first day of school, on parent night, during each and every conference, to each individual conversation, I stress the importance of working together so that I can do the very best for their child. Each letter I write ends with, "Thank you for being a partner with me in the education of your child." I remind parents that they are their child's first teacher and I will only have the opportunity to work with their child for 176 days, yet they have their child's entire life. In order for me to do my personal best, I need their support. Even though I don't always get full support, it does help in opening the lines of communication in a positive way.

While it has not been my intent to give you a definitive way to solve all of the assessment questions you've ever explored, I hope this discussion of assessment and evaluation has broadened and deepened your perspective, made it all seem more do-able, and given some practical, tangible, tried-and-true ways to look at assessment from real-life situations.

It's not about assessment either; it's about life.

For Further Study

Mathematics Assessment: Myths, Models, Good Questions, and Practical Suggestions
edited by Jean Kerr Stenmark

Expanding Student Assessment
edited by Vito Perrone

A Practical Guide to Alternative Assessment
by Joan L. Herman, Pamela R. Aschbacher, and Lynn Winters

EPILOGUE

Years ago, if anyone would have told me that I would write a book even mentioning mathematics, I would have laughed at the thought of it. But here is the book. I did it. It has been a long journey, and I have grown from being a math victim to a math appreciator. The pain and anguish of my earlier years is still there, but has been overcome with confidence, perseverance, and a desire to understand. Just like any recovery, my math phobias have been diffused "one day at a time," it didn't happen overnight.

In every experience in life, there is a lesson to be learned. A gift to be received. This book represents a collection of the many gifts I have received as I muddled my way to a greater understanding of math. Someone once said that the greatest gifts are those that are given away. I offer this book to you as my gift.

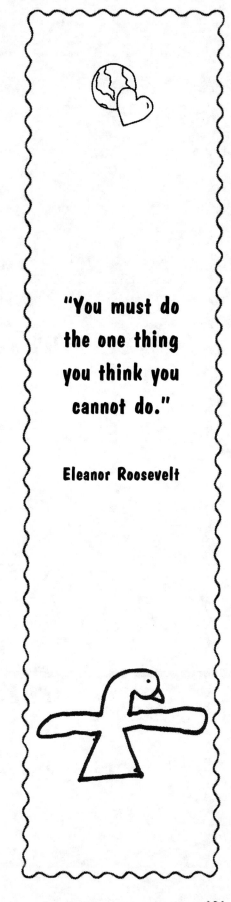

"You must do the one thing you think you cannot do."

Eleanor Roosevelt

For information regarding
workshop opportunities on

It's Not About Math, It's About Life

please contact:

Susan Kovalik & Associates

17051 SE 272nd St., Suite 17

Kent, WA 98042-4659

Phone: 253/631-4400

Fax: 253/631-7500 www.kovalik.com

To view our website on

It's Not About Math, It's About Life

please go to

www.members.aol.com/lifemath

Appendices

Graphing is as easy as *A-B-C*

A AAAAAAAAAAAAAAAAAAAAAAA

What kind of APPLE do you like?

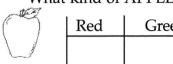

Red	Green	Yellow

B BBBBBBBBBBBBBBBBBBBBBBBBBBB

What time do you usually go to BED?

7:30	8:00	8:30	9:00	Other

C CCCCCCCCCCCCCCCCCCCCCCCCCC

What is your favorite COOKIE?

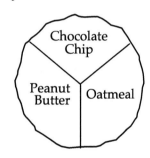

Chocolate Chip

Peanut Butter   Oatmeal

D DDDDDDDDDDDDDDDDDDDDDDDD

What kind of DONUTS do you like?

Chocolate	
Glaze	
Sprinkles	

E EEEEEEEEEEEEEEEEEEEEEEEEEEEEE

How do you like your EGGS?

Fried	Scrambled	Boiled	Yuck

F FFFFFFFFFFFFFFFFFFFFFFFFFFFFFFFFF

What's your favorite FOOD?

_____ Pizza

_____ Tacos

_____ Hamburgers

_____ Spaghetti

_____ Other_____

G GGGGGGGGGGGGGGGGGGGGGGGG

What's your favorite kind of GUM?

Big Red
Juicy Fruit
Doublemint
Bubble Gum
Other

H HHHHHHHHHHHHHHHHHHHHHHHH

How do you say "Hi"

	Howdy		Hi
	Hello		Other
	Hey		

I IIIIIIIIIIIIIIIIIIIIIIIIIIIIIIIIIIIIIIIIIIIII

What's your favorite ICE CREAM?

Vanilla
Chocolate
Strawberry
Other

204

J JJJJJJJJJJJJJJJJJJJJJJJJJJJJJJJJJJJJJJJJJJJ

Can you JUMP ROPE?

Yes	No

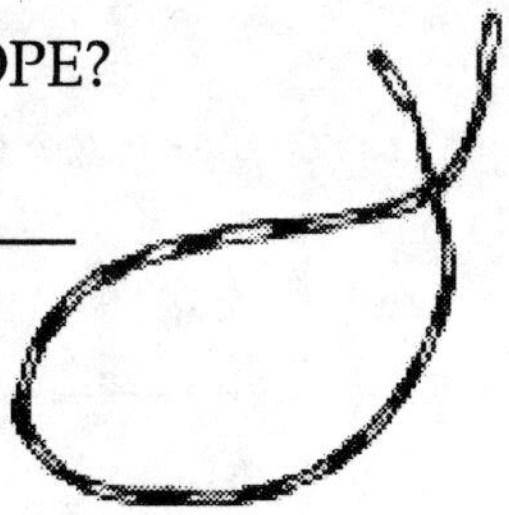

K KKKKKKKKKKKKKKKKKKKKKKKKKKK

Have you ever flown a KITE ?

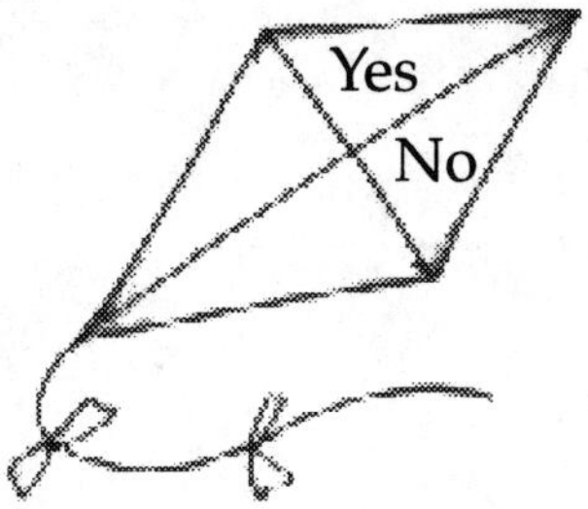

L LLLLLLLLLLLLLLLLLLLLLLLLLLLLLLLL

Does LIGHTNING scare you?

Always	Never	Sometimes

M MMMMMMMMMMMMMMMMMMMM

Do you use a MICROSCOPE?

Sometimes	All the time	Never

N NNNNNNNNNNNNNNNNNNNNNNNNNNNN

What is your favorite NUMBER?

0 1 2 3 4 5 6 7 8 9

O OOOOOOOOOOOOOOOOOOOOOOOOOO

What is your favorite kind of OLIVE?

	Green
	Black
	Yuck

P PPPPPPPPPPPPPPPPPPPPPPPPPPPPPPPPP

What kind of PIE do you like?

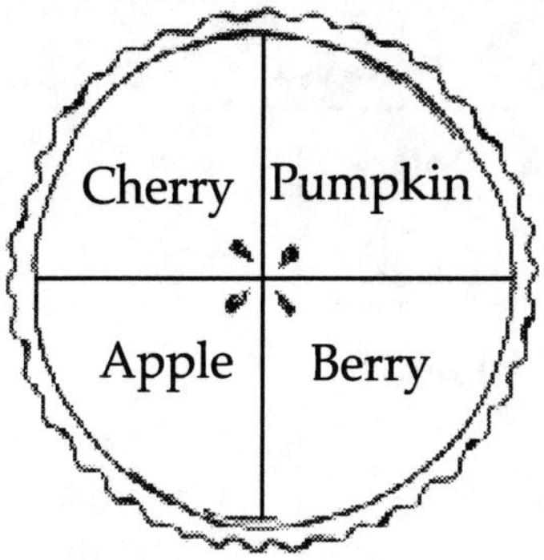

Q QQQQQQQQQQQQQQQQQQQQQQQQQ

Q is for QUILT.

Do you have one?

R RRRRRRRRRRRRRRRRRRRRRRRRRRRRRRR

Are you wearing any RED today?

Yes	No

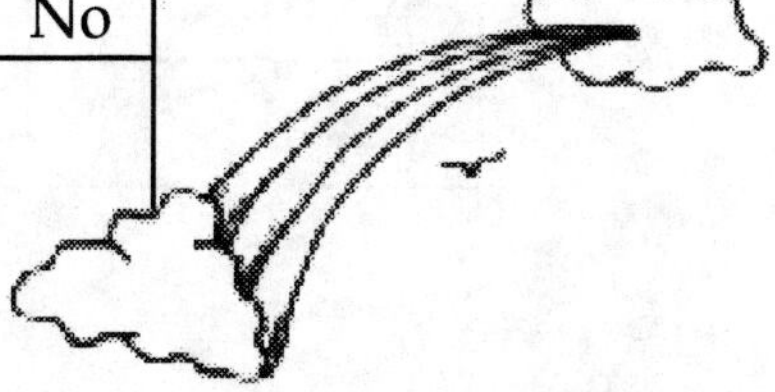

Graphing is as easy as **A-B-C** cont.

Appendix A

S SSSSSSSSSSSSSSSSSSSSSSSSSSSSSSSSS

Do you like SNAKES?

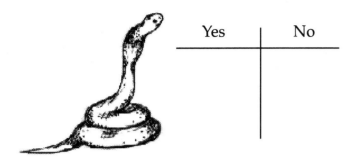

Yes	No

T TTTTTTTTTTTTTTTTTTTTTTTTTTTTTT

What's your favorite TOY?

	Doll
	Truck
	Lego
	Other _____

U UUUUUUUUUUUUUUUUUUUUUUUU

Have you ever used an UMBRELLA?

YES | NO

V VVVVVVVVVVVVVVVVVVVVVVVVVV

What's your favorite VEGGIE?

Green Beans	Peas
Corn	Tomatoes
Carrots	Other

W WWWWWWWWWWWWWWWWWWWWWWW

Have you ever had a WISH come true?

Yes	
No	

X XXXXXXXXXXXXXXXXXXXXXXXXXX

Have you ever heard a XYLOPHONE?

Yes	No

Y YYYYYYYYYYYYYYYYYYYYYYYYYY

Do you think YANKEE DOODLE was real or make believe?

Real	Make Believe

Z ZZZZZZZZZZZZZZZZZZZZZZZZZZZZ

Do you like ZIPPERS or buttons?

Zippers	
Buttons	

The behavior guidelines of the ITI learning environment, called Lifelong Guidelines, are:

TRUSTWORTHINESS:

To act in a manner that makes one worthy of confidence.

TRUTHFULNESS:

Telling the truth is about personal responsibility and mental accountability.

ACTIVE LISTENING:

Listening with intention involves more than just hearing the words.

NO PUT-DOWNS:

A put-down is a way of saying, "I am better than you, richer than you, smarter than you, have more options than you."

PERSONAL BEST, including LIFESKILLS:

Doing one's best at all times.

LIFESKILLS

INTEGRITY: To act according to a sense of what's right and wrong

INITIATIVE: To do something, of one's own free will, because it needs to be done

FLEXIBILITY: To be willing to alter plans when necessary

PERSEVERANCE: To keep at it

ORGANIZATION: To plan, arrange, and implement in an orderly way; to keep things orderly and ready to use

SENSE OF HUMOR: To laugh and be playful without harming others

EFFORT: To do your best

COMMON SENSE: To use good judgment

PROBLEM-SOLVING: To create solutions in difficult situations and everyday problems

RESPONSIBILITY: To respond when appropriate, to be accountable for your actions

PATIENCE: To wait calmly for someone or something

FRIENDSHIP: To make and keep a friend through mutual trust and caring

CURIOSITY: A desire to investigate and seek understanding of one's world

COOPERATION: To work together toward a common goal or purpose

CARING: To feel and show concern for others

COURAGE: To act according to one's beliefs

PRIDE: Satisfaction from doing your personal best

Additional Resources

Burns, Marilyn. "Writing in Math Class," *Instructor Magazine*, April 1995.

Lazear, David. *Seven Ways of Teaching: The Artistry of Teaching With Multiple Intelligences*. Illinois: IRI/Skylight Training and Publishing, 1991.

For more information or related workshop opportunities in Kovalik's ITI Model, please call Susan Kovalik & Associates 253/631-4400 or visit their web site: www.kovalik.com ITI is a comprehensive educational model that translates brain research into practical classroom strategies transforming traditional schools into lively, dynamic learning communities.

Web pages such as the following:

  www.capecod.net/wixon.htm
  www.csun.edu

Endnotes

ENDNOTES

Chapter 1 INTRODUCTION

1   Yetta Goodman, Keynote Speech at Whole Language Umbrella Conference (Phoenix, Arizona, August, 1991)

2   National Academy Press,"Everybody Counts: A Report to the Nation on the Future of Mathematics Education," National Academy Press (1989):58

3   California State Department of Education, *It's Elementary!* (Sacramento, CA: California State Department of Education), 8

4   Leslie Hart, *"Anchor" Math* (Kent, WA: Books for Educators, 1992), 32

5   Edith Biggs and James McLean, *Freedom to Learn* (New York: Addison-Wesley, 1969), 3

Chapter 2 REAL MATH VS. SCHOOL MATH

1   Michael Smith Ph.D., *Humble Pi: The Role Mathematics Should Play in American Education* (New York: Prometheus Books, 1994), 71

2   Claudia Zaslavsky, *Fear of Math: How to Get Over It and Get On With Your Life* (New Jersey: Rutgers University Press, 1994), 21

3   ibid., 137

4   ibid., 38

5   ibid., 140

6   Smith, *Humble Pi,* 68

7   *ibid.*

8   Edward MacNeal, *Mathsemantics: Making Numbers Talk Sense* (New York: Penguin, 1994), 269

8   Hart, *"Anchor" Math,* 25

9   *ibid.*

10 Zaslavsky, *Fear of Math,* 109

11 *ibid.*

12 Regan Robertson, *Number Power: A Cooperative Approach to Mathematics and Social Development* (Addison-Wesley, 1994)

13 Dr. Spencer Kagan's New Cooperative Learning, Kagan Cooperative Learning, "Smart Card" 1997.

14 Elizabeth Cohen, *Designing Groupwork: Strategies for the Heterogeneous Classroom* (New York: Teachers College Press, 1994),67-73

15 Susan Kovalik, *ITI: The Model,* (Kent, WA: Susan Kovalik & Associates, Inc., 1994), 90

16 Kovalik, *ITI: The Model,* Ch. 9

Chapter 3 WHAT IS MATH?

1   Hal Saunders, *When Are We Ever Gonna Have to Use This?* Updated Third Edition (CA: Dale Seymour Publications, 1988), i-ii

2   National Council of Teachers of Mathematics, *Curriculum and Evaluation Standards for School Mathematics* (Virginia: NCTM, 1989), 11

Chapter 4 THROUGH THE LOOKING GLASS

1   "Brain Calisthenics," *Life Magazine* (July, 1994) and "A Head for Numbers," *Discover the World of Science* (July, 1997)

2   PBS Video series, *"The Brain: Our Universe Within,"* (Discovery Channel, 1994)

3   *USA Today*, (May 13, 1992): 9

4   Robert Rivlin and Karen Gravelle, *Deciphering Your Senses* (New York: Simon & Schuster, 1984), Chapter 1

5   Karen Olsen and Susan Kovalik, *Kid's Eye View of Science: A Teacher's Handbook for Implementing an Integrated Thematic Approach to Teaching Science, K-6* (Kent, WA: Center for the Future of Public Education, 1994), 13

6   ibid., 14-15

7   ibid., 36-37

8   ibid., 37

9   Jane Healy, Ph.D., *Endangered Minds: Why Our Children Don't Think and What We Can Do About It* (Simon & Schuster, 1990), 112

10 ibid., 112

11 Leslie Hart, *Human Brain and Human Learning* (Kent, WA: Books for Educators, 1983), 56

12 Mary K. Healy and Mary Barr, *Language Across the Curriculum: Handbook of Research on Teaching Specific Aspects of the English Language Arts Curriculum*

13 Howard Gardner, *Frames of Mind: The Theory of Multiple Intelligences* (New York: Basic Books, Inc., 1985), Ch 7

14 *ibid.*, Ch.7

15 Howard Sharron, *Changing Children's Minds: Feuerstein's Revolution in the Teaching of Intelligence* (England: Imaginative Minds, 1994), 36-39

16 Stephen Hawkings, *Everybody Counts: A Report to the Nation for Educators* (1992), 35

17 Hart, *Human Brain and Human Learning*, 67

Chapter 5 LANGUAGE AND MATH

1   Healy and Barr, *Language Across the Curriculum*, 126

2   David Berliner and Ursula Casanova, *Putting Research to Work in Your School* (New York: Scholastic, 1993), 5

3   MacNeal, *Mathsemantics*, 37

4   Sonia Helton, "You Can Count On It!" (Internet: "Gold Files," 1992)

5   MacNeal, *Mathsemantics*, 94

6   Healy and Barr, *Language Across the Curriculum*, 112

7   JoAnne Oppenheim, *The Elementary School Handbook: Making the Most of Your Child's Education* (New York: Pantheon Books, 1989), 127

8   National Council of Teachers of Mathematics, *NCTM Addenda Series* (Virginia: NCTM, 1989), 6

9   Hart, *"Anchor" Math*, 4

10 Jean Kerr Stenmark, *Mathematics Assessment: Myths, Models, Good Questions and Practical Suggestions* (Virginia: NCTM, 1991), 48

11 Healy and Barr, *Language Across the Curriculum*, 112

12 Marilyn Burns, *"Writing In Math Class? Absolutely!"* Instructor Magazine (April 1995): 40

13 Sonia Helton, "You Can Count On It"

Chapter 6 MATH AND TECHNOLOGY

1   NCTM, *Curriculum and Evaluation Standards for School Mathematics*, 6

2   Robert Sylwester, *A Celebration of Neurons: An Educator's Guide to the Human Brain* (Virginia: ASCD, 1995), 195

3   ibid., 121

4   ibid., 121

5   NCTM, *Curriculum and Evaluation Standards for School Mathematics*, 8

6   Mark Share, (Phoenix, Arizona, 1996)

7   Apple Classrooms of Tomorrow Level Self-Evaluation—Project EXCEL, Creighton School District (Phoenix, Arizona, 1996)

8   Sylwester, *A Celebration of Neurons*, 121

Chapter 7 GIRLS AND MATH—GENDER EQUITY

1 Susan McGee Bailey, "Shortchanging Girls and Boys," *Educational Leadership* (May 1996): 75

2 ibid., 75

3 Mary Piper, Ph.D, *Reviving Ophelia: Saving the Selves of Adolescent Girls* (New York: Ballantine Books, 1995), 63

Chapter 9 PRACTICAL APPLICATIONS—THEME MATH

1 Robert Ellingsen, *Classroom of the 21st Century* (Kent WA: Books for Educators, 1989), 58

2 The Earthworks Group, *50 Simple Things Kids Can Do To Save The Earth* (New York: Scholastic, 1990), 26-27, 29, 36, 38, 42

3 Linda Allison, *Blood and Guts* (New York: Scholastic, 1992)

4 Lawrence Mound, *Eyewitness Juniors Book: Amazing Insects and Amazing Butterflies and Moths* (New York: Alfred A. Knopf, 1993), 8, 9, 16, 18, 27

5 Susan O'Connell, "Connecting the Mathematics Classroom to the World," *Teaching Children Mathematics, Volume 1, Number 5* (January, 1995): 268

6 Ellingsen, *Classroom of the 21st Century*, 58

Chapter 10 MATH CHALLENGES IN THE REAL WORLD

1 City of Phoenix Aviation Department, *Economic Impact Phoenix Airport System Book*, (Phoenix, AZ: City of Phoenix Aviation Department), 4

2 ibid., 1-24

3 *NCTM Addenda Series*, 6

Chapter 11 MICRO—COMMUNITIES

1 "Kid's Town, USA" (Nevada: Jacobson Elementary School, 1996)

Chapter 12 DAILY MATH OPPORTUNITIES IN THE CLASSROOM

1 Hart, *"Anchor" Math*, 126

2 Martin Lee and Marcia Miller, *Great Graphing* (New York: Scholastic, 1993), 5

3 Braddon, Hall, and Taylor, *Math Through Children's Literature* (Colorado: Teacher Ideas Press, 1993), 3

4 National Academy Press, *Everybody Counts: A Report to the Nation on the Future of Mathematics Education* (Washington, D.C.: National Academy Press, 1989): 57

Chapter 13 MATH AT HOME—A GUIDE TO ASSIST PARENTS

1   Jacqulyn Saunders with Pamela Espeland, *Bringing Out the Best: A Resource Guide for the Parents of Young Gifted Children* (Minneapolis: Free Spirit Press, 1986)

2   Jean Kerr Stenmark, *Family Math* (California: Regents of UC, 1986), 19-20

Chapter 14 ASSESSMENT

1   Lorrie Shepard, "Why We Need Better Assessment," *Educational Leadership*, (April, 1989)

2   Vito Perrone, *Expanding Student Assessment* (Alexandria: ASCD, 1991), Adapted from Figure 2.2, 28

3   ibid., 31

4   J. Herman, P. Aschbacher, and L. Winters, *A Practical Guide to Alternative Assessment* (Virginia: ASCD, 1992), 8

5   Stenmark, *Family Math*, 35

6   Stenmark, *Family Math*, 36

7   Renate and Geoffrey Caine, *Making Connections: Teaching and the Human Brain* (Addison-Wesley, 1991), 166

Bibliography

BIBLIOGRAPHY

Allison, Linda. *Blood and Guts.* New York: Scholastic, 1992.

Aschbacher, H. and L. Winters. *A Practical Guide to Alternative Assessment.* Virginia: ASCD, 1992.

Bailey, Susan McGee. "Shortchanging Girls and Boys," *Education Leadership.* May, 1996.

Berliner, David and Ursula Casanova. *Putting Research to Work In Your School.* New York: Scholastic, 1993.

Biggs, Edith and James McLean. *Freedom to Learn.* New York: Addison-Wesley, 1969.

Braddon, Hall & Taylor. *Math Through Children's Literature.* Colorado: Teacher Ideas Press, 1993.

Burns, Marilyn. "Writing in Math Class? Absolutely!" *Instructor Magazine.* April 1995.

Caine, Renate and Geoffrey. *Making Connections: Teaching and the Human Brain.* New York: Addison-Wesley, 1991.

California State Department of Education. *It's Elementary!* Sacramento, CA.

City of Phoenix Aviation Department. *Economic Impact Phoenix Airport System Book.* Phoenix, AZ

Clawson, Calvin C. *Conquering Math Phobia: A Painless Primer.* New York: John Wiley & Sons, Inc., 1991.

Cohen, Elizabeth. *Designing Groupwork: Strategies for the Heterogeneous Classroom.* New York: Teachers College Press, 1994.

Ellingsen, Robert. *Classroom of the 21st Century.* Kent, WA: Susan Kovalik & Associates, Inc., 1989.

Flansberg, Scott ("The Human Calculator") and Victoria Hay, Ph.D. *Math Magic.* New York: William Morrow Publishers, 1993.

Gardner, Howard. *Frames of Mind: The Theory of Multiple Intelligences.* New York: Basic Books, Inc., 1985.

Hart, Leslie. *"Anchor" Math.* Kent, WA: Books for Educators, 1992.

Hart, Leslie. *Human Brain and Human Learning.* Kent, WA: Books for Educators, 1983.

Hawkings, Stephen. *Everybody Counts: A Report to the Nation for Educators.* 1992

Healy Ph.D., Jane. *Endangered Minds: Why Our Children Don't Think and What We Can Do About It.* New York: Simon & Schuster, 1990.

Healy, Mary K. and Mary Barr. *Language Across the Curriculum: Handbook of Research on Teaching Specific Aspects of the English Language Arts Curriculum.*

Helton, Sonia. "You Can Count On It!" Internet: "Gold Files,"1992.

Herman, Joan L., et al. *A Practical Guide to Alternative Assessment.* Alexandria, VA: ASCD, 1992.

Jacobson Elementary School. "Kid's Town, USA." Las Vegas, Nevada.

Kappan Journal. "Teaching Children Mathematics." January, 1995.

Kovalik, Susan. *ITI: The Model, Third Edition.* Kent, WA: Susan Kovalik & Associates, Inc., 1994.

Lee, Martin and Marcia Miller. *Great Graphing: More Than 60 Activities for Collecting, Displaying, and Using Data.* New York: Scholastic, 1993.

MacNeal, Edward. *Mathsemantics: Making Numbers Talk.* New York: Viking Penguin, 1994.

Mound, Lawrence. *Eyewitness Juniors Book: Amazing Insects and Amazing Butterflies and Moths.* New York: Alfred A. Knopf, 1991.

National Academy Press. *Everybody Counts: A Report to the Nation on the Future of Mathematics Education.* Washington, D.C.: National Academy Press, 1989.

National Council of Teachers of Mathematics. *Curriculum and Evaluation Standards for School Mathematics.* Virginia: NCTM, 1989.

O'Connell, Susan. "Connecting the Mathematics Classroom to the World," *Teaching Children Mathematics, Volume 1, Number 5.* January, 1995.

Olsen, Karen and Susan Kovalik. *Kid's Eye View of Science: A Teacher's Handbook for Implementing an Integrated Thematic Approach to Teaching Science, K-6.* Kent, WA: Center for the Future of Public Education, 1994.

Oppeneheim, Joanne. *The Elementary School Handbook: Making the Most of Your Child's Education.* New York: Pantheon Books, 1989.

Paulos, John Allen. *Beyond Numeracy: Ruminations of a Numbers Man.* New York: Alfred A. Knopf, 1991.

PBS Video series. "The Brain: Our Universe Within." Discovery Channel, 1994.

Perrone, Vito, editor. *Expanding Student Assessment.* Alexandria, VA: ASCD, 1991.

Piper, Mary, Ph.D. *Reviving Ophelia: Saving the Selves of Adolescent Girls.* New York: Ballantine Books, A Division of Random House, Inc., 1995.

Bibliography

Polonsky, Lydia, et al. *Math for the Very Young: A Handbook of Activities for Parents and Teachers.* New York: John Wiley & Sons, Inc., 1995.

Rivlin, Robert and Karen Gravelle. *Deciphering Your Senses.* New York: Simon & Schuster, 1984

Robertson, Regan. *Number Power: A Cooperative Approach to Mathematics and Social Development.* New York: Addison-Wesley, 1994.

Saunders, Hal. *When Are We Ever Gonna Have To Use This? Updated Third Edition.* Palo Alto, CA: Dale Seymour Publications, 1988.

Saunders, Jacqulyn with Pamela Espeland. *Bringing Out The Best: A Resource Guide for the Parents of Young Gifted Children.* Minneapolis: Free Spirit Press, 1986.

Sharron, Howard. *Changing Children's Minds: Feuerstein's Revolution in the Teaching of Intelligence.* England: Imaginative Minds, 1994.

Sheppard, Laurie. "Why We Need Better Assessment." *Educational Leadership.* April, 1989.

Smith, Ph.D., Michael. *Humble Pi: The Role Mathematics Should Play in American Education.* New York: Prometheus Books, 1994.

Stenmark, Jean Kerr. *Family Math.* CA: Regents of UC, 1986.

Stenmark, Jean Kerr, editor. *Mathematics Assessment: Myths, Models, Good Questions, and Practical Suggestions.* Reston, VA: National Council of Teachers of Mathematics, 1991.

Sylwester, Robert. *A Celebration of Neurons: An Educators Guide to the Human Brain.* Virginia: ASCD, 1995.

The Earthworks Group. *50 Simple Things Kids Can Do to Save the Earth.* New York: Scholastic, 1990.

Tobias, Sheila. *Overcoming Math Anxiety, Revised and Expanded.* New York/London: W.W. Norton & Company, 1993.

Troutman, Andria P. and Betty K. Lichtenberg. *Mathematics, A Good Beginning: Strategies for Teaching Children, 4th Edition.* Pacific Grove, CA: Brooks/Cole Publishing Co., 1991.

USA Today, May 13, 1992.

Zaslavsky, Claudia. *Fear of Math: How to Get Over It and Get On With Your Life.* New Jersey: Rutgers University Press, 1994.